ANTI WOKE

SELECTED ESSAYS BY BRENDAN O'NEILL

connorcourt
PUBLISHING

Published in 2018 by Connor Court Publishing

Copyright © Brendan O'Neill

Connor Court Publishing Pty Ltd
PO Box 7257
Redland Bay QLD 4165
sales@connorcourt.com

www.connorcourtpublishing.com.au

Phone 0497 900 685

ISBN: 9781925826265

Cover design: Ian James

Printed in Australia

For Bill

CONTENTS

1

KATY PERRY'S HAIR

Katy Perry has made a public apology. She's been filmed making a *mea culpa*. She has confessed to having made 'several mistakes' in recent years. What exactly were her moral crimes? Did she get embroiled in a drug scandal? Is she a tax-dodging queen? Did her spat with Taylor Swift cross the line from tweets to violence?

Nope. She once wore her hair in cornrows.

The 'cultural appropriation' hysteria has reached such a fever pitch that celebs are now apologising for hairstyles. In an interview with DeRay McKesson, Black Lives Matter activist and host of the podcast *Pod Save The People*, Perry fessed up to her many 'mistakes', including sporting cornrows in the video for her song *This Is How We Do* and rocking the geisha look at the 2013 American Music Awards. In the world of the cultural-appropriation fanatic, who frowns viciously upon any borrowing from a culture other than one's own, such behaviour is tantamount to blacking-up and singing 'Mammy'.

Perry has now learned the lesson of her crazy foray into arrogant white-lady cultural theft. 'Why can't I wear my hair that way?', she asked herself when *This Is How We Do* caused a Twitter-stink. Luckily for her, 'empowered angels' — BS-speak for politically correct people — were on hand to give her an answer. It's because there is 'power in black women's hair' and white women can't just steal that.

Acknowledging that her whiteness means she will never fully grasp this mystery of black women's hair-related power, Perry says she is nonetheless trying to redeem herself for her crimes against cultural purity. 'I will never understand, but I can educate myself, and that's what I'm trying to do', she told McKesson.

This act of moral self-flagellation confirms how widespread the cultural-appropriation panic has become. When even someone as pop as Perry, who has more Twitter followers than most countries have citizens, is playing the awful game of bowing and scraping before cultural dividing lines, you know PC madness has gone mainstream.

Will other celebrities follow suit? Will Beyonce finally apologise for that time she wore a sari, which *Teen Vogue,* fashion mag turned mouthpiece of PC silliness, held up as proof that India is treated as 'a shallow vessel that exists for Westerners to find themselves'? Will black actress Zoe Saldana beg forgiveness for using darkening make-up to make herself a little blacker for the role of Nina Simone, which one mag branded an act of black appropriation whose 'degree of wackness… cannot be overstated'? And how about Ke$ha, who in the video for her song *Crazy Kids* wears not only cornrows but also a grill and enough bling to make Mr T blush? Surely it's the stocks for her.

The clampdown on cultural appropriation has gone crazy. Campuses forbid the wearing of sombreros lest Mexicans feel culturally violated. Britain's Glastonbury music festival has banned the sale of Native American headdress. Authors are warned against writing characters of a different race or culture to them, which I'm pretty sure would make the entire enterprise of literature impossible, or at least pointless.

Anthony Horowitz, British author of the wildly popular *Alex Rider* teen novels, was advised not to include a black character in his latest story because that is 'not [your] experience'. Imagine if all authors wrote only from personal experience. All of Shakespeare's plays would be about people who grew up the sons of glove-makers in sleepy Stratford. More importantly, the very humanity of literature, its capacity for finding the universal in the particular, for uncovering some of the truth of human life across the racial, gender and sexual board, would be destroyed.

The aim of the sanction against cultural appropriation is actually quite sinister. It is to keep us in our cultural lanes. It is to lock us into our racial boxes. It's a plea for cultural purity, a rehashing, in PC lingo, of that dark, old 20th-century idea that biology or heritage should count for more than our shared humanity, and that blacks and whites will never really understand each other. Don't mix, it says. It rehabilitates segregation, or at least the segregationist imagination. 'I will never understand', as Perry said. That is, she will never understand black people. How depressing is it that this has become an acceptable and even media-praised thing to say in the 2010s?

'I will never understand' is the cry of the right-on in the 21st century, and it runs directly counter to every properly liberal, enlightened movement of the past hundred years, which encouraged understanding, solidarity in fact, across the racial divide.

The new celebration of cultural purity deadens culture. It drains pop culture in particular of the thing that keeps it alive and urgent and sometimes brilliant: its fusions and rip-offs and derivations. Pretty much every form of popular entertainment we enjoy is a product of cultural mixing, whether it's rock, springing from the interactions of blacks and whites in the American South, or hip-hop, which in the early days nodded to 1970s European electro music, or Western blockbuster movies, which have borrowed from the style and feel of East Asian cinema. At the high-art level, Shakespeare and Chaucer borrowed most of their stories from other authors. All culture is 'cultural appropriation'. Cultural appropriation isn't some terrible evil — it's the stuff of art and entertainment and life itself.

How awful that Perry is communicating to her young fanbase the idea that it's bad to borrow from other cultures. Why is she doing this? Well, there's the rub. It's because while white self-flagellation might look like self-hatred, it is in fact, darkly ironically, a new shortcut to the moral high ground. It's how you show you're 'woke'. And everyone wants to be woke now, wokeness being that 'perceived sense of intellectual superiority and enlightenment' the chattering classes claim to enjoy, in the words of the *Urban Dictionary*. Anti-white self-flagellation is how you prove you're a Good White Person in contrast with white trash who wear chunky jewellery and speak in black twangs or college students who think it's okay to don a sombrero.

Whether it's Perry apologising for her cultural crimes, Macklemore rapping about his white privilege, or Lena Dunham bemoaning her own 'privileged white womanhood', modern culture is stuffed with white folks beating themselves up. But their self-ridicule is really an advert for their white wokeness. So not only does the cultural-appropriation hysteria racially compartmentalise humanity and agitate against the creation of new and potentially brilliant forms of mixed-up art, it also creates the space for rich whites to show how switched-on they are in comparison with us the rabble. Everything about it is terrible.

2

BIG BROTHER

It's great to see that leftists and millennials and others are snapping up George Orwell's *Nineteen Eighty-Four* in a bid to make some sense of Donald Trump's presidency. Because when they get deep into this dystopian tale — into the Newspeaking, sex-fearing, history-rewriting meat of it — they might realise that it describes their authoritarianism far better than Trump's. I can picture their faces now: 'Guys, wait... is this novel about us?'

The book shot to the top of Amazon's bestseller list after Kellyanne Conway used the phrase 'alternative facts' to describe the Trump administration's belief that the crowds at his inauguration were larger than the media had let on. People pointed out that 'alternative facts' sounds creepily like something the Party in Orwell's story would say. Trump seems to believe he can fashion facts from thin air, to boost his own political standing.

'Alternative facts is a George Orwell phrase', said *Washington Post* reporter Karen Tumulty. MSNBC correspondent Joy Reid tweeted the following lines from the novel: 'The Party told you to reject the evidence of your eyes and ears. It was their final, most essential command.' Within hours *Nineteen Eighty-Four* was a bestseller again, people buying it as a map to the liberty-challenging Trump era.

But the novel is a better guide to what preceded Trump, to the nannying, nudging, speech-policing, sex-panicking, PC culture that Trumpism is in many ways a reaction against.

Consider the Junior Anti-Sex League, the prudish youths in Orwell's story who think the 'sex impulse' is dangerous and who devote themselves to spying on interactions between the sexes. 'Eroticism was the enemy', they believed. 'Desire was thoughtcrime.' If this prissiness finds its echo in anyone today, it isn't in the creepily oversexed, pussy-grabbing Trump — it's in the stiff buzz-killers of the campus feminist movement.

These radical wallflowers demonise drunk sex, bossily insisting that all sexual interactions must be 'sober, imaginative, enthusiastic, creative, wanted, informed, mutual and honest'. (Even the Junior Anti-Sex League didn't come up with such a thorough list of what counts as acceptable sex.) They drag male students to campus kangaroo courts for allegedly doing sex the wrong way. Student officials in Britain have banned the making of 'animal noises' in the student bar lest they arouse sexual bravado in men, and sexual dread in women.

Fortunately, it is curable. Some universities make freshmen undergo diversity training, inculcating them with the correct mindset on all matters sexual, racial and social. The University of Delaware, going full O'Brien (O'Brien was the torturer in Orwell's novel), referred to its diversity training as 'treatment' for incorrect attitudes. *The New York Times* reported last year that more and more students think diversity training 'smacks of some sort of Communist re-education programme'. The modern campus, as devoted to treating moral infection as it is to imparting knowledge, could adopt O'Brien's cry as its slogan: 'Shall I tell you why we have brought you here? To cure you!'

And of course there's thoughtcrime. The Party punishes anyone who dares to hold a point of view it disagrees with. Not unlike modern PC warriors who will brand you a 'denier' if you're not fully eco-conformist, and a 'misogynist' if you criticise feminism, and a phobe (Islamophobe, transphobe, homophobe) if you deviate from various PC orthodoxies.

Witness the doublespeak of today's leftist lovers of censorship. They create Safe Spaces, they speak of 'the right to be comfortable'. These are darkly Orwellian euphemisms for censorship. The Party would be proud of these people who have successfully repackaged the expulsion of unpopular views as 'safety' and 'comfort'; who will use actual threats and force to secure students' 'safety' against unpleasant ideas. War is Peace, Violence is Safety, Censorship is Comfort.

And how about Newspeak, the Party's made-up, minimalist language that it pressures people to adopt? That finds expression today in the Pronoun Police, who demonise the use of 'he' and 'she' as potentially transphobic and invent Newspeak pronouns in their stead. Some campuses now want everyone to use 'ze' as a default pronoun. 'Ze' might be the most Newspeak word ever: a strange small word you must use if you want to be considered morally good.

Then there is the war on history, the demolition of ugly or inconvenient historical ideas and symbols. In *Nineteen Eighty-Four*, old things that have fallen out of favour are plunged down the memory hole. Today, PC zealots demand the tearing down of statues of old colonialists or the renaming of university halls that are named after people from the past who — shock, horror — had different values to ours. The Year Zero fervour of Orwell's

Party is mirrored now in the behaviour of intolerant PC culture warriors.

Trump has authoritarian impulses, that's for sure. But his is a clumsy authoritarianism, oafish rather than Orwellian. In *Nineteen Eighty-Four*, leftists and millennials won't find a dystopian, fictionalised version of Trumpism — they'll find themselves. In the Party, in the treatment of ideas as disorders, in the Two Minutes Hate against those who are offensive or different, in the hounding of unpopular opinions, in the memory-holing of difficult things, they will see their own tragic creed reflected back to them. They will find a stinging rebuke from history of their own embrace of the sexless, joyless, ban-happy urge to control almost every area of individual thought and life. I hope they heed this rebuke, and change.

Reason, 10 February 2017

3

SAINT HILLARY

If you want to see politics based on emotionalism over reason and a borderline-religious devotion to an iconic figure, forget the Trump Army — look instead to the Cult of Clinton.

Ever since Donald Trump won the presidential election, all eyes, and wringing hands, have been on the white blob who voted for him. These 'loud, illiterate and credulous people', as a sap at *Salon* brands them, think on an 'emotional level'. Bill Moyers warned that ours is a 'dark age of unreason', in which 'low information' folks are lining up behind 'The Trump Emotion Machine'. Andrew Sullivan said Trump supporters relate to him as a 'cult leader fused with the idea of the nation'. There's now a widespread view, or rather prejudice, that says anyone who voted for Trump was behaving viscerally rather than rationally.

What's funny about this fear and loathing for Trump and his voters is not only that it's the biggest liberal-elite hissy fit of the 21st century so far — and liberal-elite hissy fits are always funny. It's that whatever you think of Trump (I'm not a fan) or his supporters (I think they're mostly normal, good people), the fact is they have got nothing on the Clinton Cult when it comes to creepy, pious worship of a politician.

By the Cult of Hillary Clinton, I don't mean the nearly 65million

Americans who voted for her. I have not one doubt that they are as mixed and normal a bag of people as the Trumpites are. No, I mean the Hillary machine — the celebs and activists and hacks who were so devoted to getting her elected and who have spent the months since her loss sobbing and moaning about it. These people exhibit cult-like behaviour far more than any Trump cheerer I've come across.

Trump supporters view their man as a leader 'fused with the idea of the nation'? Perhaps some do, but at least they don't see him as 'light itself'. That's how Clinton was described in the subhead of a piece for Lena Dunham's *Lenny Letter*. 'Maybe [Clinton] is more than a president', gushed writer Virginia Heffernan. 'Maybe she is an idea, a world-historical heroine, light itself.' Nothing this nutty has been said by any of Trump's media fanboys.

'Hillary is Athena', Heffernan continued, adding that 'Hillary did everything right in this campaign… She cannot be faulted, criticised, or analysed for even one more second.'

That's a key cry of the Cult of Hillary (as it is among followers of L Ron Hubbard or devotees of Hare Krishna): our gal is beyond criticism, beyond the sober and technical analysis of mere humans. Michael Moore, in his movie *Trumpland*, looked out at his audience and, with voice breaking, said: 'Maybe Hillary could be our Pope Francis.'

Or consider comic Kate McKinnon's post-election opening bit on *Saturday Night Live*, in which she played Clinton as a pantsuited angel at a piano singing Leonard Cohen's 'Hallelujah', her voice almost cracking as she sang: 'I told the truth, I didn't come to fool ya.' Just imagine if some right-leaning Christian celeb (are there any?) had dolled up as Trump-as-godhead and sang praises to him. It would have been the source of East Coast mirth for years to come. But *SNL's* 'Hallelujah' for Hillary was seen as perfectly normal.

As with all saints and prophets, all human manifestations of light itself, the problem is never with them, but with us. We mortals are not worthy of Hillary. 'Hillary didn't fail us, we failed her', asserted a writer for the *Guardian*. The press, and by extension the rest of us, 'crucified her', claimed a columnist at *Bustle* magazine. We always do that to messiahs, assholes that we are.

And of course the light of Hillary had to be guarded against blasphemy. Truly did the Cult of Hillary seek to put her beyond 'analysis for even one more second'. All that stuff about her dodgy emails and her role in the Libya disaster was pseudo-scandal, inventions of her aspiring slayers, they told us again and again.

As Thomas Frank says, the insistence that Hillary was scandal-free had a blasphemy-deflecting feel to it. The message was that 'Hillary was virtually without flaws... a peerless leader clad in saintly white... a caring benefactor of women and children.' Mother Teresa in a pantsuit, basically. Such was the slavish media devotion to Hillary, wrote Frank, that during the election, and in its aftermath, 'the act of opening a newspaper started to feel like tuning in to a Cold War propaganda station'.

Then there was the reaction to Clinton's loss. It just wasn't normal behaviour. '"I feel hated", I tell my husband, sobbing in front of the TV in my yoga pants and Hillary sweatshirt, holding my bare neck', said a feminist in the *Guardian*. Crying was a major theme. A British feminist recalled all the 'Clinton-related crying' she had done: 'I've cried at the pantsuit flashmob, your *Saturday Night Live* appearance, and sometimes just while watching the debates.' (Wonder if she cried over the women killed as a result

of Hillary's machinations in Libya? Probably not. In the mind of
the Hillary cultists, that didn't happen — it is utterly spurious, a
blasphemy, beyond analysis.)

Then there was Lena Dunham, who came out in hives — actual
hives — when she heard Clinton had lost. Her party dress 'felt tight
and itchy'. She 'ached in the places that make me a woman'. Eurgh.
I understand being upset and angry at your candidate's loss, but this
is something different; this is what happens, not when a politician
does badly, but when your saviour, your Athena, 'light itself', is
extinguished. The grief is understandable only in the context of the
apocalyptic faith they had put in Hillary.

It was all incredibly revealing. What it points to is a mainstream,
Democratic left that is so bereft of ideas and so disconnected from
everyday people that it ends up pursuing an utterly substance-
free politics of emotion and feeling and doesn't even realise it is
doing that. They are good, everyone else is bad; they are light itself,
everyone else is darkness; and so no self-awareness can exist and no
self-criticism can be entertained. 'Not for even one more second.'
The Cult of Hillary Clinton is the clearest manifestation yet of the
21st-century problem of life in the political echo chamber: you
come to view yourselves as gods and others as devils.

Mercifully, some *mea culpas* emerged. Some, though not enough,
realised that Hillaryites behaved rashly and with unreason. In a
piece titled 'The unbearable smugness of the liberal media', Will
Rahn recounted how the media allowed itself to become the earthly
instrument of Clinton's cause, obsessed with finding out how to
make Middle Americans 'stop worshiping their false god and accept
our gospel'.

Indeed. And the failure to make the gospel of Hillary into the actual book of America points to the one good thing about Trump's victory: a willingness among ordinary people to blaspheme against supposed saints, to reject phoney saviours, and to turn against the new secular religion of hollow progressiveness. The liberal political and media establishment offered the little people a supposedly flawless, Francis-like figure of uncommon goodness, and the little people called bullshit on it. That is epic, a sign of the confidence and optimism in the new populist public mood that is sweeping the West.

Reason, 20 November 2016

4

BLOODY WHITE PEOPLE

In the freakish universe of identity politics, there is surely no creature sadder than the self-hating white person. All it takes for these people to be engulfed by existential angst is a glimpse in the mirror. Or a shiny shop window. And there it is, looking back at them: their pasty pallor, their bleached features, a grim reminder that they were born and remain marked with the original sin of whiteness.

You can spot a white self-hater from miles off. They always look stressed out — being a member of literally the worst race that ever existed will do that to you. They might sport a Black Lives Matter badge, but they'll rip it off faster than you can say 'whitesplaining' if a black person tells them to stop appropriating his politics.

They write tweets that begin with 'Dear White People...' and go on to list all the things white folks must stop doing: wearing dreadlocks, eating jerk chicken, asking black people about their hair. These are 'microaggressions'. It is proof of whitey's inherited imperial arrogance that he thinks he can steal black people's culture and taunt them with queries about where they got their hair cut as if he was still 'masta'.

And they're forever checking their privilege. This is what all good honkies must do. It's a 21st-century version of self-flagellation. Only instead of beating themselves across the back with nettles, these self-race-baiters attend things like 'The White Privilege Conference' (that's a real thing in the US), to gab about such matters as 'How to Collectively Heal the Cycle of White Supremacy'. I think I'd rather the nettles.

There was an outburst of this bizarro racial self-hatred in Australia recently. When *Meanjin*, the literary quarterly, defaced its logo by turning the 'Me' bit into '#MeToo' and scribbling out the rest, all hell broke loose. Well, Twitter went into meltdown.

'Meanjin', you see, is the Turrbal word for the land that became Brisbane. So these literary luvvies were erasing an Aboriginal slogan to make way for a feminist one, unwittingly opening a Pandora's Box of identitarian bitching and competitive grievance. It was virtue-signalling gone wrong — hilariously wrong — with *Meanjin's* people saying, 'Look at us and how much we care about wimmim!', only for the Twitterati to turn around and say, 'Guys, why do you hate the First Nations?'

It didn't take long for *Meanjin's* editorial staff to come up with an explanation for their heinous act of graphic-design genocide — it was their whiteness that made them do it! Of course it was. Bloody whiteness. Always causing trouble.

So *Meanjin* editor Jonathan Green begged for clemency from Twitter's kangaroo court (no linguistic violence intended by my use of the word kangaroo). He pleaded that his 'casual obliteration of a proud Indigenous word' was a 'reminder of my privilege' and how 'blind' that privilege has made him to other people's suffering. He means his white privilege, naturally, that black mark — agh — that all white people bear.

Two of the pained white ladies who had articles in the #MeToo *Meanjin* — Clementine Ford and Anna Spargo-Ryan — went one better than Green on the back-whipping front. They issued a statement acknowledging 'the deep hurt' caused by the cover ('to seven people on Twitter', they could have added, but didn't).

'As white women', they continued, really trotting out today's fashionable racial inferiority complex, 'we want to recognise that this [cover] is precisely part of the ongoing trauma caused by whiteness in this country'.

They said they would donate their *Meanjin* fee to a charity that works with Aboriginal women. Let's call this what it is: a Catholic-style indulgence, the offering of money to reduce the amount of punishment one must undergo for one's sin. Crikey, these people are now doing actual penance as part of their grovelling apologetics for their skin colour.

If *Meanjin*'s editorial staff had a single funny bone between them — which they don't: humour is anathema to these agonised apologisers for historic hurt — they would have defaced the follow-up issue so that the 'Me' in 'Meanjin' became 'Mea culpa' and devoted the whole bloody thing to pretend-apologising for the ridiculous notion that drawing a line through a word is a crime against humanity.

I mean, seriously, how low does your opinion of Aboriginal people have to be for you to believe they will be mortally mentally wounded by the editorial decisions of a journal read by some university professors and the Melbourne macchiato set?

This is what happens when you think hyper-racially, as the left now does, in alarming contrast to earlier leftists who said 'Let's be colourblind, guys': you resuscitate racial stereotypes. It's one of the great ironies of white self-loathing: in positing whiteness as all-powerful, even trauma-inducing, and black people as bundles of nerves liable to feel 'deep hurt' over a magazine cover, this poisonous PC creed actually rehabilitates the old skewed relationship between whites and blacks. Whites are the adults and so must always watch their words, especially around blacks, who are apparently the children: easily harmed by off-colour comments. How grotesque.

Ford and Spargo-Ryan don't realise that it wasn't their writing for the #MeToo *Meanjin* that made them appear racist — it was their presumption of fragility on the part of Aboriginal women, and their belief that they, as upstanding white women, must throw cash at these Aboriginal women as compensation for their psychic pain. The racism was in their apologism, not in *Meanjin*.

This small, awful affair reveals that white self-loathing has actually become a highly coveted accessory among PC whites. This is the weird thing about anti-white white people: there's a boastfulness to their self-loathing. They want as many people as possible to see just how much they hate their accidental racial make-up. And that's because this white shame is in fact a new version of white pride. These people are signalling to the world that they are good whites: aware, switched-on, not like those other whites, the uncouth, uneducated ones. They beat themselves up, yes, but to the narcissistic end of making a fat public spectacle of their heightened sensitivity.

So they demean blacks by depicting them as permanent victims, and they divide whites into Good and Bad. Can identity politics get any nastier?

The Spectator, 9 June 2018

5

OSAMA THE ENVIRONMENTALIST

So Osama bin Laden was an environmentalist. In between plotting the mass murder of kaffirs and dreaming of the destruction of the West, he penned teary-eyed missives about the dangers of 'catastrophic climate change'. Coming off like an earnest member of Greenpeace who had read one too many Naomi Klein tracts, he wrote a letter in 2009 calling on Americans to do everything within their power to 'save humanity from the harmful gases that threaten its destiny'.

Released by the Obama administration in March 2016, the letter says mankind is living in 'the shadow of catastrophic climate conditions' and we need a 'revolution' to make the planet cleaner. If you read the letter out at the next IPCC gathering, you'd probably get a rousing round of applause.

Some people seem freaked out to discover that OBL had green tendencies. How is it possible that this finger-wagging lunatic could have been as one with the West's own respectable chattering classes on the issue of climate change? One columnist seems perturbed that bin Laden had what he describes as a more 'progressive' take on climate change than the current Republican Party.

But why the surprise? It makes perfect sense that this anti-Western, anti-modern medieval throwback should have warmed to green thinking. After all, bin Laden's biggest beef in life was that the modern West was an overly cocky, supremely destructive entity that needed to be taken down a peg or two — which is exactly what environmentalists think, too.

Bin Laden's 2009 letter, written to coincide with the coming to power of Obama, is not the first time he got moist-eyed about manmade planetary doom. In 2002 he attacked the US for pursuing progress at the expense of poor, sad Mother Earth. 'You have destroyed nature with your industrial waste and gases more than any other nation in history', he hectored, like an agitated hippie.

Hilariously, he lambasted President George W Bush for 'refus[ing] to sign the Kyoto agreement' on climate-reduction targets. There's something deliciously surreal about a terrorist outlaw who was then running from hideout to hideout lecturing the president of the United States for failing to sign on the dotted line of a global treaty.

In 2007 he lectured the foul, greedy West again, claiming that 'all of mankind is in danger because of the global warming resulting to a large degree from the emissions of the factories of the major corporations'. He beat Occupy Wall Street to the punch by four years, slamming the 'greed and avarice of the major corporations and their representatives'.

Then, in the 2009 letter, released in 2016, he outlined his solution to all this Western wickedness: 'The world should put its efforts into attempting to reduce the release of gases.' In a nutshell, join Greenpeace. Take eco-action. Put pressure on corporations. Bin Laden basically had two feelings about the American people: that they should die or, failing that, become dutiful warriors against climate change.

Greens are understandably peeved to discover OBL was a fellow worrier about climate change. Well, how would you feel if you found out that the 21st century's worst terrorist shared your moral outlook? Some try to skirt the severe awkwardness of finding themselves in the same bed as bin Laden by claiming he was being accidentally 'progressive'. Indeed, in response to the recently released bin Laden letter, a writer for *Fusion* magazine analysed the Republican presidential candidates' attitudes toward climate change and found that all of them are 'less progressive than Osama bin Laden when it comes to [this] global threat'. So in worrying about manmade climate change, bin Laden was being decent for a change, more decent than some of America's own politicians.

There is nothing mysterious about OBL's longstanding attraction to the politics of environmentalism, from his 2002 plea to America to sign up to Kyoto to his 2009 call for a 'revolution' in eco-attitudes. He seems simply to have recognised that his innate anti-Westernism, his violent agitation with what he viewed as the sins and crimes of modernity, could be expressed through green miserabilism as well as through his main pursuit of Islamo-terrorism.

He was a voracious consumer of lefty Western thought — quoting both Noam Chomsky and Robert Fisk and constantly droning on about the evilness of corporations — and it seems that one of the strains of lefty Western thought he liked best was climate-change alarmism, the idea that the West has become so industrially and politically arrogant that it now threatens the whole of mankind. The ugly, polluting West will bring about 'the death and displacement of millions of human beings', he once said.

With its misanthropic streak, its anti-Americanism, its

discomfort with modernity, and its instinct to return the world to a simpler, pre-modern state, it isn't hard to see why environmentalism made OBL's ears prick up. If 9/11 was a declaration of war on American hubris, then OBL's later green-leaning statements were a continuation of that war by other means: they were a green-tinted restatement of the apocalyptic barbarism and anti-modernism of 9/11 itself.

Greens can kid themselves all they like that bin Laden's many eco-statements were just a case of his being accidentally, or opportunistically, 'progressive'; but in truth they are an awkward reminder of the fundamentally regressive nature of environmentalism, a creed so against progress that even this chief agitator against the modern West could find succour in it.

National Review, 2 March 2016

6

DEFYING NATURE

I love technology. I love technology because it has made human life so much better than it was. In the time since Jesus skulked the Earth, the human population has grown from 180million people to seven billion. Most of that growth in numbers took place over the past hundred years. Life expectancy has rocketed upwards, from a global average of 28 back then to around 70 today. We are taller, fitter, brainier and freer than we have ever been.

All of these advances are a result of what we call technology. They are a result of our transformation of the Earth, our efforts to make this weird watery planet more hospitable to humanity, our exploitation of nature for the benefit of mankind. Because if you look back at human history and ask yourself the question, 'What is technology?', you will see that it is, in essence, the conquering of nature with tools. Technology is the means through which we squeeze more out of Mother Earth than she is prepared to give us.

We have used tools such as ploughs, scythes, axes, compasses, shovels, ships, spaceships, drills and machinery in order to sow, reap, mine, explode, smelt, build and fly. Technology represents our defiance of nature. Nature creates a canyon, we build a bridge; nature forgets to give us wings, we invent the aeroplane; nature refuses to tell us what uranium is good for, we experiment with it anyway and create a technology that can light up entire cities. Technology is the clearest expression of mankind's cockiness, his refusal to live only on those few secrets nature is willing to share with him.

How different it is today. Today, many of the new technologies do not express anything like the pioneering spirit; instead they are tools for narcissism. Much technology today is not about taming the world around us — it is about obsessing over our inner worlds, our own emotions and fleeting feelings. New technology does not encourage us to 'go forth and multiply'; it encourages us to stay home and navel-gaze. Where technology was once a tool for exploration, today it is a tool for retreat. The most serious problem with the new technologies is not that they invite us to lead busy and frenetic lives, but that they invite us to be meek and unambitious, to become estranged from the old ideals of outward human endeavour.

Ours is an era in which there is extraordinary hostility towards any technology that tampers with nature, alongside a wild, almost demented celebration of new technologies that allow us to preen and pamper ourselves. So drilling for oil or digging for coal – despite using some of the most remarkable technology created by man – is frowned upon, seen as the equivalent of raping Gaia. Say the words 'nuclear power' to the average member of the chattering classes and watch him splutter on his macchiato. 'Dam' is now a far dirtier word than 'damn', despite the fact that dams represent one of the high points of human technology, the mastery of vast waterscapes for the purpose of providing water and electricity to millions upon millions of people. All of those technologies are high up on the list of the opinion-forming classes' least favourite things.

Meanwhile, new technologies which allow for greater communication or for hours of shallow self-reflection are championed. The iPhone is worshipped. Facebook and Twitter enjoy an extraordinary level of cultural validation, although there has lately been controversies over their political influence and the space they provide for wicked or questionable people to spout wicked or questionable views. The internet is seen as a great invention, give or take a few downsides, such as its Nigerian spammers and rampant pornography.

Planet-altering technologies are demonised. Mood-altering technologies are celebrated. Technologies that change the physical world around us, which force nature to reveal her secrets, are seen as evil. Technologies which allow us to retreat into a virtual world, to take refuge from physical realities in a universe of chat and blather, are seen as good.

Indeed, today we have the curious situation where activists utilise new technologies as part of their war against what they consider to be outdated old technologies. So, posh environmentalists use their iPhones and iPads to organise campaigns against flying, particularly against 'cheap flights' and other white-trash activities which they regard as harmful to the planet. Greenpeace makes full use of the internet to spread its unhinged propaganda about the dangers of nuclear power and oil exploration. In some quarters, the new technologies have been turned into weapons against the old idea that technology should remake the world according to humanity's needs and in humanity's image.

Technology was once concerned with humanising the planet, with increasing the human footprint. So-called new technologies are largely about shrinking the human footprint. From wind power to quieter aeroplanes to electric cars to Skype-based international conferences – many of the new technological breakthroughs are about reining in humanity, limiting his impact on his surroundings, making him a good virtual creature rather a bad physical one. Because the more virtual we become, the less destructive we can be.

In essence, the new technologies facilitate our retreat from making history. They cater to our backward desire to shrivel up and hibernate rather than to explore and expand. Of course, it isn't the technology's fault. And of course, the internet and mobile communications are potentially wonderful, world-connecting things – just because some people use technology in a weird way, that doesn't mean that technology is 'bad'.

But we do get the technologies we deserve. So in the 16th and 17th centuries, when the human spirit of exploration was strong, we got vast ships capable of traversing entire oceans that had terrified earlier generations. In that postwar positive moment of the 1950s we got nuclear power and the space race. And today, at a time of great human meekness and fear and risk-aversion and eco-panic, we get technologies that allow us to hide from the world and to hide from our responsibility to make history. We get technologies that allow us to reflect obsessively on ourselves rather than to reflect on our relationship with the Earth, and with the future.

The real problem with the new technologies is that they mould themselves around, and indeed flatter, modern man's extraordinary levels of historic laziness and lack of ambition. Where once we defied nature, now we defy our own deeply human instinct to venture into the world, to treat the Earth, in Christopher Lasch's words, as 'an empty wilderness to be shaped to our own design'.

Speech at the Wilderness Festival in Oxfordshire, 13 August 2011

7

THE GLAMOUR OF TRAUMA

Rhodes Must Fall, the gang of spoilt Oxford brats who want a statue of the colonialist Cecil Rhodes removed from Oriel College, is being chalked up as another outburst of campus craziness. The media are having a field day mocking the hypocrisies and idiocies of the Rhodes-fearing students, one of whom is a Rhodes scholar — so he'll take Rhodes' cash but doesn't want to look at his likeness — and all of whom describe walking past the statue as 'an act of violence'. At a time when students complain that doing yoga is 'cultural appropriation' and reading Shakespeare can trigger PTSD, Rhodes Must Fall is being viewed as the latest loopy pursuit of bookish youth who inhabit a different moral universe to the rest of us.

But to treat Rhodes Must Fall in this way is to miss a trick. For this movement is in fact infused with some very mainstream ways of thinking. The true engine of Rhodes Must Fall is the culture of victimhood, the view of the self as a hapless object to which things happen, upon which wicked words wreak havoc, a creature easily propelled into trauma by ideas or images or experiences. And that's an idea which exists far beyond the quad of Oriel College, Oxford. Indeed, for all their pretences to radicalism — ironically fuelled by a media that treat them as extreme and exceptional — the Rhodes Must Fall people only express in gruff, Year Zero-style terms what is now one of the key, and most depressing, outlooks of the 21st-century West.

It is of course tempting just to slam the Rhodes Must Fall brigade. They typify today's super-sensitive students, who fear the content of books and claim to be 'triggered' by the arrival on campus of anyone who has a different point of view to theirs. So they describe the statue of Rhodes as 'aggressive'. They claim this stone representation of a man who plundered Africa 'harms' black students. As I argued in a piece for *Newsweek*, Rhodes Must Fall is ISIS-like, sharing with those statue-smashing Islamists 'a Year Zero attitude, a desire to rewrite history… to cleanse all remnants of a "problematic" past from the present'. This is the irony of today's students who pose as caring: their flipside is a desire to destroy with extreme prejudice any idea or icon that offends them. They're wimpish and tyrannical at the same time.

Yet Rhodes Must Fall is not some out-there group. It is better seen as just a rougher expression of an everyday culture: the cult of the victim. The most striking thing about the Rhodes Must Fall activists is their self-negation of their moral autonomy, their reduction of themselves to mere products of history, created and damaged by historical circumstance and their cultural surroundings as surely as cells in a petri dish are rearranged by a scientist. They claim the statue of Rhodes does 'violence' to them. They say they are victims of 'the colonial wound'. They argue that 'the festering, rotting wound that is the ideology of white supremacy' continues to do damage to 'our black and brown bodies'.

Here, black students — intelligent, autonomous people — are

reduced to mere 'bodies', shoved and shaped by the inanimate representations of history that surround them. One supporter of Rhodes Must Fall says it is unacceptable to have such 'cultural detritus of empire' on campus, as it can be 'stifling for non-white students', speaking to how history 'continues to harm black and minority-ethnic people living in Britain today'. The irony of a supposedly anti-racist movement treating black students effectively as bovine, as less capable than whites of negotiating public life or controversial spaces, as easily 'acted upon' by long-gone events, is as profound as it is dispiriting: in seeking to speak up for blacks, it actually diminishes their autonomy, their humanity.

What is most notable about Rhodes Must Fall is its treatment of history as a source of psychological trauma. Its supporters refer to the 'invisible violence' that is done to them — invisible because it isn't actually happening — and talk about the 'wound' of history. Dr Omar Khan, director of the race think-tank the Runnymede Trust, argues that 'seeing Rhodes so recognised [causes] a deep wound that isn't merely in people's heads nor in any way irrational'. That is, it literally wounds them, as a knife might.

This depiction of history as a wounding thing speaks to today's cult of self-victimisation, the deep 21st-century urge to define oneself as a victim of circumstance rather than a shaper of destiny. Because the students who make up Rhodes Must Fall are among the most comfortable, cosseted young people in Western Europe, enjoying the extraordinary privilege of reading and thinking in one of the world's oldest, most prestigious universities, they must trawl the past in search of victim status. Unable to find anything unpleasant in their cushioned lives, they instead plunder the suffering of earlier black generations in order to discover some hurt they might claim as their own. These are the very students most likely to complain about 'cultural appropriation', yet they engage in a most foul form of what we might call historical appropriation: they claim to feel the pain of the enslaved and the colonised as they sip tea in the swooning towers of Oxford. It would be like me demanding a ban on images of potatoes on the basis that they make me feel the stabbing hunger pains of my ancestors who perished in the Irish Famine.

What we're witnessing is the rise of the transcendental victim, the victim who steals the long-passed pain of his ancestors or even of the dead with whom he has no connection whatsoever. Rhodes Must Fall isn't alone in this. There's now such a thing as second- and third-generation Holocaust survivors, the children and grandchildren of those who survived the Nazi death camps, who claim to experience Nazi-related 'trauma'. Supporters of the slavery reparations movement claim it's really hard for black people today to 'endure this historical inhumanity'. This cynical use of history to construct a victim identity can also be seen in radical Islamism: Western Muslim youth claim to be motivated by anger over the Crusades, while al-Qaeda, ISIS and others talk endlessly about events of a thousand or more years ago. What ultimately binds the supposed leftists of Rhodes Must Fall with extremist Islamist youth is a cloying self-pity, an invented victim identity, a belief that society and history have conspired to insult them.

At a time of great misanthropy, when individuals' capacity for autonomy is called into question and the idea of free will is ridiculed, Western society has come to value the easily harmed individual who demands therapy and recognition of his suffering over the self-motored, morally independent individual who believes that he can cut it by himself, with a little help from his friends, comrades and community. And in such a climate, those who lack victim status, those who aren't actually suffering, must hunt down insults, exaggerate sights, and build a case for their being wounded creatures equally deserving of social sympathy and state resources. We are actively incited to play the victim. This explains everything from the obsession with 'microaggressions' to feminists' obsessive logging of normal behaviour as 'everyday sexism' to Oxford students' depiction of a statue as violence: it's all an attempt to construct victimhood and thus win respect. This is the glamour of trauma, the desire to deck oneself out in the finery of weakness, which is, bizarrely, the most prized look among today's morally emaciated bourgeoise.

Strikingly, Rhodes Must Fall says it is engaged in the 'politics of recognition', demanding that Oxford and others 'recognise' the 'effacement and violence' historically faced by blacks. This isn't an anti-establishment movement; on the contrary, it is a craven, knee-bent plea for the new establishment — the victim-therapeutic complex — to confer victim-legitimacy on middle-class black students who lack it. In an earlier era when the ideal of autonomy was more respected, individuals demonstrated their mettle by taking responsibility for their lives and being driven; in today's climate of victim sacralisation, individuals are encouraged to play down their own moral resources, to disavow their own humanity, in essence.

So, yes, we can laugh at Rhodes Must Fall. We should, in fact. But to do only that would be to overlook the powerful anti-human trends infusing such a movement. More people must refuse to play the victim game, to strip themselves of moral independence in the hope of gaining recognition from a victim-obsessed state and society, and instead insist that they are not 'bodies' hurt by history, but rather are minds and hands that might make history. History doesn't simply happen to us; we happen to history, too.

spiked, 28 December 2015

8

RELIGIOUS INSTRUCTION

As someone who attended faith schools from the ages of four to 18 — and also a faith nursery, faith youth club, faith swimming lessons, faith teenybopper discos, faith football matches, and faith outings to the seaside — I find the commentariat's fear of these institutions fascinating. Nothing freaks out today's privately educated ragers against religion quite as much as a school where the teachers talk to the children about God. They need to calm down, because the real secret about faith schools, the hidden truth, is that they more often produce intellectual sceptics than mental slaves.

Some people look upon faith schools as alien institutions, the churners-out of brain-raped youngsters who will hate homos and want to strangle single mums. '[W]e have no idea what children are being taught in those classrooms', says Catherine Bennett in *The Observer*, providing her readers with their weekly satisfying shudder at the thought of how the strange sections of society live. These schools 'brainwash impressionable children', the *New Statesman* warns, quoting that old Jesuit boast, 'Give me the child until he is seven and I will give you the man', as evidence.

Arch New Atheist Richard Dawkins, like a bull in a Padre Pio bookshop, caused the Bimonthly New Atheist Controversy — it's like they have a contract with the papers — by saying faith schools should not be given 'a free pass to do religious education in their own way' and must be prevented from 'indoctrinating' children. He was promoting his scary-sounding Channel 4 show, *Faith School Menace?*

There are at least three problems with this sport of Hate The Faith School. First, there's the insulting idea that the kids are being brainwashed. Are the social circles of the liberal, atheistic, PC classes really so narrow that they have never met anyone who attended a CofE, Jewish, Muslim or Catholic school? They mustn't have, because if they had they would know that the idea that faith-school children have their minds turned to mush by all-powerful priests, rabbis and imams is hilarious.

Take my school. (Warning: anecdotal evidence ahead.) A convent-based school in a rundown part of North-West London, administered by Dominican sisters who saw it as their duty to beat — sometimes literally — us Catholic boys and girls into shape, it was fairly full-on, religious-wise. We prayed before lessons, read the Bible, raised money for black babies, had a chapel. (I say chapel. It was more of a glorified shed, which, being made of wood, got badly damaged in the Great Storm of 1987.)

But were we Pope-fearin' Stepford kids? Far from it. Me and a friend beheaded a statue of St Vincent de Paul. The school Bibles were awash with cartoon penises sticking out of Jesus of Nazareth's smock and speech bubbles above the apostles' heads saying, 'I am gay'. In flagrant defiance of priestly teachings, a legend scrawled on the walls of the boys' toilet said: 'Wanking is evil / Evil is a sin / Sins are forgiven / So get stuck in.' In their own little way, those four lines pose a serious theological challenge to the many contradictions of the Catholic faith.

What the faith-school fearers forget is that, yes, 12-, 13-, 14- and 15-year-olds are wet behind the ears and sometimes dumb, but they also don't believe everything they are told. They are developing a sceptical streak, which in 13-year-old boys might express itself crudely in the agonising cry 'What do you mean I can't masturbate?!', but which nonetheless speaks to an inner questioning of supposed big truths.

When a teen is told that everything from bodily pleasure to playground arguments to wanting to be super-wealthy is sinful, he will instinctively recognise a contradiction between his desires and what is expected of him. This often leads, not to brainwashing, but to an instinct to 'kick against the pricks' (to quote Acts, Chapter 9, Verse 5).

Indeed, in my experience, people who have been to faith schools often have a natural scepticism towards spiritual crackpots. Perhaps all those years ingesting, considering and often rejecting religious instruction strengthens our bullshit immune system. Everyone I know who attended a Catholic school is now an atheist, an agnostic, a lapsed Catholic or a pretend Catholic (someone who attends Mass only so that his or her child will get into a Catholic school, giving rise to what we might call fake-faith schools). Meanwhile, it is often the trendily and liberally educated who later in life most feverishly embrace New Ageism, Buddhism Lite, or end-of-the-world environmentalism. Suckers. Some of us had done that whole finding God and losing Him again by the time we were halfway through puberty.

The second problem with the fashion for bashing faith schools is that it is seriously, properly illiberal. The idea, expressed by Dawkins and others, that educating a child in a religious faith is a form of 'emotional abuse' is really an attack on the right of parents to raise their children as they see fit. In an Oxford Amnesty lecture that is very popular among the New Atheist set, one militant secularist argued that children 'have a human right not to have their minds crippled by exposure to other people's bad ideas'. An intolerant campaign run by the British Humanist Association seeks to bring faith schools to an end, in the name of children's freedom of belief.

This is an Orwellian use of the language of 'freedom', for it is really an attack on adults' freedom of association, on parents' freedom to get together with whomever they please in order to share ideas and find the education system they feel is right for their children. As Hannah Arendt, a far more profound thinker than today's New Atheists, argued in the late 1950s, to 'force parents' to send their children to a particular school against their wishes means 'to deprive them of rights which clearly belong to them in all free societies — the private right over their children and the social right to free association'. Campaigning for the government to shrink the faith element in faith schools would force some parents into precisely this scenario.

And thirdly, in answer to Catherine Bennett's hair-tearing question about what on earth is taught in faith schools, the truth is they teach the same curriculum as every other school — they have to — and, sadly, they increasingly teach the same PC nonsense as every other school, too. Catholic schools, for example, teach far less of the anti-sex, pro-God stuff and far more about environmentalism, multiculturalism, identitarianism and other brands of 21st-century tripe. My old school recently won a Friends of the Earth award for being super-green by sticking a solar panel on the roof and getting the children to recycle their rubbish. Not surprisingly, none of the brave warriors against faith schools have a word to say about children being 'indoctrinated' in these meek, fearful, self-loathing pieties of the new liberal zeitgeist. I just hope the kids one day do to their recycling bins what I did to St Vincent de Paul.

spiked, 3 November 2016

9

STOP WATCHING PORN

The trouble with criticising the relentless rise of porn, the poking of appendages and orifices from pretty much every computer screen on Earth, is that people will think you're a prude.

So what a relief that a genuine libertine — Pamela Anderson — has slammed porn as a losers' game, and argued that its colonisation of the internet, its march into the gadgets permanently attached to our non-wanking hand, speaks to a new reluctance to engage in the 'ample rewards of healthy sexuality'. Yes, the former *Baywatch* star, awakener of a million teenage boys' sexuality, has come out as porn-sceptic, and given the critique of porn the injection of respectability it needed.

Anderson has teamed up with Shmuley Boteach, an Orthodox Jewish rabbi, TV presenter and author of such books as *Kosher Sex: A Recipe for Passion and Intimacy*. Their message is simple: guys, and girls, stop using porn so much. They veer too closely to pseudo-scientific scaremongering about porn, describing it as having 'addictive dangers' — when in fact even the hand-knackered 15-year-old lad could stop watching muck if he really wanted to — and fretting over the 'devastation' that 'porn addiction' wreaks on society. But away from their tendency to hyperbole, they make strong points. 'Porn is for losers', they insist. It is a 'boring, wasteful and dead-end outlet for people too lazy to reap the ample rewards of healthy sexuality'.

They're right. The rise of porn-use fundamentally represents a turn away from the 'ample rewards' of actual sex, of taking a risk with another living, breathing being. Loads of explanations have been put forward for the industrialisation of porn, but none has been convincing. It speaks to the continued stranglehold of male entitlement over society, say feminists, which makes zero sense at a time when women in the West are leaving their male counterparts for dust in school, Uni and the workplace (under the age of 30 at least). It shows our young are out of control, perverted, say religious warriors against porn, which would be more convincing if survey after survey didn't suggest that yoof are squarer than ever, drinking less and smoking less and fretting over mortgages more than any young adults in history. No, the rise of porn is not an expression of patriarchal arrogance or a sign of perversion among the young; rather, it reflects a broader retreat from intimacy, a growing conviction in the modern West that losing yourself in another person, physically or emotionally, is a risky business, best avoided.

Porn has filled the gap — if that isn't too graphic a metaphor — left by the crisis of human intimacy. Anderson and Boteach get at this when they brand porn a pastime of those 'too lazy' to 'reap the rewards' of sex. Although 'lazy' is the wrong word; it's more like too fearful. A cowardice in relation to other people is the fuel of the porn industry. Ours is an era that treats sexual intimacy as a minefield, something likely to disease you or damage your mental esteem. From the great AIDS panic, with its depiction of 'unsafe sex', the most intimate form of sex, as a kind of raunchy Russian roulette, to those public-health campaigns that tell us our fellow citizens are less people we might want to know carnally and more walking incubators of CHLAMYDIA or GONORRHOEA, we're constantly advised to see sex as too great a physical risk. And then there is its emotional toll. From the classroom to popular culture to the publishing world's new cash cow — New Feminist tracts — the message we're bombarded with is that intense intimacy can be damaging, especially for women, especially for the young. So play it cool. Keep your distance.

Nothing better speaks to the anomie of the 21st century, to the other-people allergy that underpins the politics of fear, than the problematisation of intimacy. It's now so bad that respectable sections of society actually promote masturbation as a healthy alternative to the madness of a sexual encounter. The National Health Service tells young people that masturbation is 'basically sex by yourself' — if you think that's sex, you've been having some bad sex — and chirps that there are 'few risks involved: you can't get pregnant or catch a sexually transmitted infection from wanking'. Schools teach about the virtues of masturbation. Numerous 'sexpert' books on bashing the bishop push it as an attractive alternative to romantic passion, with all 'the pain and the hurt and the suffering' such passion involves. The new cult of self-love, of massaging both your genitals and your self-esteem, speaks profoundly to a retreat from engagement, from humanity.

And we wonder why there are so many wankers. People are positively encouraged to wank. Indeed, it would be wrong today to see the porn industry as some deviant, outlier gang, infecting society with filth; it is better seen as the militant wing of an utterly mainstream fear of sexual intimacy, making mileage, and money, from the anomie running through the West today. There's a dark irony to feminists' hatred of the porn industry: in contributing fairly significantly to the demonisation of intimacy, to the culture of fear that now surrounds relations between the sexes, feminists, among others, paved the way for this new industry that fetishises sex, that offers a readymade performance of sex through which gratification can be achieved without 'the pain and the hurt and the suffering' of engagement.

This is where Anderson and Boteach get their emphasis slightly wrong: the problem is less that porn is corrupting society, and more that the already existing corruption of our society, and of the ideal of intimacy, helped to nurture the industry of porn. The crisis of intimacy has led to a fetishisation of sex, as spotted by Christopher Lasch 40 years ago in his classic book *Culture of Narcissism*. Western societies increasingly 'make a virtue of emotional disengagement', he said, and this can lead to a 'desire to divest [sex] of the emotional intensity that unavoidably clings to it'. Four decades on, aided by the spread of the internet, sex divested not only of intensity but of human contact altogether has become the new norm. Listen to Pam: this isn't good. But to fix it, it isn't enough to rage against porn, far less to ban it; no, we need to challenge the cultural war on intimacy and its unwitting creation of an army of wankers.

spiked, 5 September 2016

10

SEXUAL MCCARTHYISM

#MeToo has officially entered its McCarthyism stage. The ousting of Ian Buruma from the *New York Review of Books* is confirmation, for those who still needed it, that this hashtag movement is more about vengeance and censorship than justice. For Buruma's crime was not to touch a woman without her consent or verbally harass his female workforce. It was merely to publish an essay by a man (Canadian broadcaster Jian Ghomeshi) who was accused of sexual assault and then acquitted in a court of law. When an esteemed editor can be expelled from polite society for publishing the words of a man who has not been found guilty of any crime, you know we live in dark times. #MeToo is the midwife of this medieval-style policing of dissenting speech.

More than any other incident so far, the Buruma affair sums up the illiberal excesses and outright hysteria of the #MeToo moment. Buruma's speechcrime was twofold. First, he dared to give space to Ghomeshi to write about the accusations made against him and, sin of sins, even to make some jokes about today's sexually straitened climate that is chewing up and spitting out men like him. Ghomeshi, who was accused by various women in 2014 of having non-consensual 'rough sex' with them — accusations that either didn't make it to court or, in the cases of three women, were thrown out of court — says in his *NYRB* piece that he is a victim of 'mass shaming'. And secondly, Buruma gave an interview to *Slate* in which he said Ghomeshi's previous behaviour is not 'really my concern'.

For this — for commissioning an essay and defending the right of an individual to continue to have a public presence after he has been acquitted of criminal offences — Buruma has been driven out of New York's literary circle. He has been hounded out because he dared to suggest we need nuance in the discussion about sexual misdemeanours and harassment. Nuance is tantamount to a sin in the binary moral universe of the #MeToo witch-hunt. One of the things that most outraged feminists is that the cover of the *NYRB* that featured Ghomeshi and others mulling over #MeToo ran with the headline 'The fall of men'. That is ridiculous, men-pitying tripe, they said — even as they helped to bring about the fall of Buruma. Buruma's fall, for mere editorial daring, proves his cover story was all too apt.

This affair confirms that any questioning of #MeToo is not allowed. Witness also the rage against Matt Damon, Sean Penn, Catherine Deneuve, and comedian Norm Macdonald, all of whom simply uttered heretical doubts about this new movement in which men can be cast out of work and into the shadows of shame simply upon the accusation of one woman. Macdonald made the blasphemous comment that it is about time the #MeToo movement 'slowed down a little bit' and the even more sinful suggestion that the likes of Louis CK — the comic whose career was destroyed following accusations that he masturbated in front of some women — should be allowed to come back. Shortly after uttering these heresies, Macdonald was due to appear on *The Tonight Show*, but he pulled out after producers told him to make a public apology for his comments at the start of the show. Publicly retract your comments, or else — what century is this?

The Macdonald and Buruma incidents show how difficult it is for public figures to criticise #MeToo. And in turn, they show how necessary it is to criticise #MeToo. Any movement that becomes this arrogant, this punishing of challenge or rebuke, must be urgently subjected to the light of serious, reasoned debate. Sean Penn was dead right to express 'suspicion' of a movement that is consumed by 'great stridency and rage' and which is 'without nuance'. 'And even when people try to discuss it in a nuanced way, the nuance itself is attacked', he said. This is precisely what happened to Buruma: he was expelled from literary society for calling for nuance. Nuance is not allowed in the #MeToo era. You must simply point and scream and revel in people's downfall.

The truth is that Buruma, in keeping with his intellectual output of recent decades, was making a very humanist argument. His comments to *Slate* were taken out of context. Everyone referred to his remark that Ghomeshi's previous behaviour is 'not really my concern'. What he actually said was: 'I'm no judge of the rights and wrongs of every allegation. How can I be? All I know is that in a court of law he was acquitted, and there is no proof he committed a crime.' Here, Buruma did something very civilised: he refused to act as a one-man mob and conspire in the permanent exclusion of Ghomeshi from public life, because he prefers to believe that individuals are innocent until proven guilty. And Ghomeshi has not been found guilty. Of anything. It used to be considered socially conscientious to treat acquitted people, and even ex-cons, fairly and humanely. Now it is seen as a social crime. #MeToo wants everyone who is merely accused to be punished forever. That is a nasty, Stalinist and utterly unjust approach to public life. Buruma is defending the pillars of the free, civilised society; #MeToo is attacking them.

Not content with conflating everything from a hand on the knee and actual rape; not content with presenting women as the frail victims of male wickedness; not content with instituting a situation where accused individuals can lose their careers and in some cases their lives (there have been four #MeToo-related suicides) — now #MeToo wants to shut down criticism, shut down nuance. Buruma shouldn't have been ousted — he should have been cheered, for he helped to start a very important discussion about the dire impact #MeToo is having on freedom, justice and sex. We should defend the #MeToo heretics before it's too late. Before we end up in a world where anyone who wants a job in journalism, culture, politics or entertainment is first asked: 'Are you now or have you ever been a critic of #MeToo?'

spiked, 20 September 2018

11

WOMEN LIE

I have found myself wondering if today's feminists, if they had been around 60 years ago, would have worn badges saying: 'I Believe Carolyn Bryant.'

Carolyn Bryant, later Carolyn Dunham, is the white woman who in August 1955 accused a young man called Emmett Till of sexually harassing her. She said Till entered the grocery store in Mississippi that she worked in and touched her without her consent. Apparently he said, 'How about a date, baby?'. When she walked away, he apparently followed her, put his arm around her waist, and said: 'What's the matter baby?'

What happened after this alleged incident is one of the darkest moments in modern American history.

Ms Bryant told people she had been sexually harassed by Till, a black boy, then just 14 years old. He had made her feel sexually vulnerable, she said. And these people hunted Till down and murdered him. They beat him, shot him, and dumped his body in a river.

This horrific crime lives on as a terrible stain on the American conscience. The photograph of Till's mutilated corpse galvanised

Americans — black and white — to change their society. And so was the civil-rights movement born.

Of course, no modern feminist would support such a barbaric act of racist violence. And yet they would have presumably believed Ms Bryant's accusations. After all, according to modern feminists, women never lie about such serious issues as sexual harassment. As reflected in the widely shared hashtag of #IBelieveHer, today's feminists encourage uncritical acceptance of all — literally all — accusations of unwanted sexual attention.

So American feminists have recently been wearing badges saying: 'I Believe Christine Blasey Ford.' Ford is the woman who has made accusations of sexual harassment against Brett Kavanaugh, Donald Trump's pick to join the US Supreme Court. Ford, a professor of psychology, alleges that 36 years ago Kavanaugh, then just 17 years old, held her down and grinded against her. Kavanaugh says this never happened. But #MeToo activists have said they believe Ford. They always believe women. Instant belief in accusations of sexual assault has become a central feature of modern feminism.

As the feminist commentator Melissa Silverstein says, 'There are a few fundamental beliefs that I hold... one of them is that I believe women'. Kneejerk belief is the meat of #MeToo. One of the most vocal leaders of #MeToo — actress turned activist Rose McGowan — recently instructed the media to stop using the word 'alleged'. 'I would challenge the media to stop using the word "alleged"', she said. This is the 'first time in history women are being believed', she continued, and the word 'alleged' only encourages doubt. A feminist reporter agreed with McGowan that 'the qualifier "alleged" should be removed from the media parlance'.

In short, every accusation made by a woman against a man should be presumed to be gospel. This is why feminists believe everything Ford said. And by the same token, they would have believed Carolyn Bryant. She claimed she had been sexually harassed. She said she had been victimised by a male. The truth, right? I believe Carolyn Bryant, yes?

Well, that would have been a moral error — a serious moral error. For Ms Bryant later admitted to a professor of history that her accusations had been false. In 2017, she told Timothy B Tyson, a professor at Duke University, that on the matter of Till being 'sexually crude' towards her, 'that part was not true'.

In short, she lied. And someone suffered, unimaginably, as a result.

Of course, Kavanaugh runs no risk of enduring what the young Till endured at the hands of racist scum. But the principle — or lack of principle — that guided their belief in the accusations of sexual impropriety against Till is the same one that guides 21st-century feminism. Namely, that women must be believed. Always. They never lie. They never misremember.

The extent to which instant belief has become a central feature of contemporary culture was captured in a headline at NBC News in the US at the end of last year. 'Why Are We Still Teaching To Kill A Mockingbird In Schools?', it said. The piece claimed that Harper Lee's classic — long the moral anchor of American education — is now problematic because it 'complicates the modern "believe victims" movement'. Virtually everyone knows that Lee's novel tells the story of siblings Scout and Jem and their dad Atticus, a lawyer who defends Tom Robinson, a black man accused of raping a white woman called Mayella. But Mayella lies. It was her who made sexual advances towards Tom, for which she was punished by her father, and so she and her father concoct a story about Tom raping her. Atticus encourages people to disbelieve Mayella. And in the current climate of instant belief, that is bad. Really bad. Atticus, in today's view, is a misogynist.

Letting schoolgirls read this book will fuel their 'growing suspicion that people don't believe girls who say they have been raped', says the NBC piece. It makes us think there is 'reason to doubt' rape accusers.

But there is reason to doubt — surely? Of course, everyone who makes an accusation of sexual assault — or of any kind of crime — should be treated sympathetically and openly. We should aspire to believe them. But we should also be sceptical. Indeed, the civilised principle of innocent until proven guilty — which is what Lee was defending — demands scepticism.

It demands that we insist on proof before we rush to condemn an individual — whether it is Emmett Till or Brett Kavanaugh. It doesn't matter if it is a lowly black youth or a Supreme Court nominee: a principle is a principle, and everyone deserves the presumption of innocence.

Today's rush to believe is bad for everyone. It is bad for men, because it threatens to condemn them before they have been justly tried. It is bad for justice, because it rubbishes key ideals of due process. And it is bad for women, too. As Margaret Atwood recently said, 'Women are human beings, with the full range of saintly and demonic behaviours this entails'. They are 'not angels'.

Indeed. Women lie, just like men do. Or they forget, like men do. Instant belief in women actually infantilises women. Worse, it is an invitation to lie. If we believe every accusation of sexual impropriety, we encourage women to use such accusations as weapons. To use them to defeat their opponents. Is that really the world we want to live in? I don't. I would rather live in a world of scepticism than credulity.

I would rather live in a world in which what happened to Emmett Till — instant punishment following instant belief — can never, ever happen again.

The Australian, 29 September 2018

12

A MANIFESTO FOR HERESY

It is my sincerely held belief that a man can never become a woman. That no matter how many hormones he takes, or operations he has, or fabulous outfits he buys, a person who was born male can never become female.

I accept a man can be a trans-woman. I accept the right of every man to claim to be a woman. And to change his name to a woman's name, if he likes. And these trans-women should of course enjoy the same rights as every other citizen: the right to vote, the right to free speech, the right to work. But to my mind, they are not women. The slogan 'Trans women are women' is a lie. This is my sincerely held belief.

Recently, this belief has become virtually unutterable in respectable society. It has become tantamount to heresy. To deny that men can become women is the modern equivalent of denying that a wafer of bread and a cup of wine became the flesh and blood of Christ during Mass. If you deny the magic of transgenderism, you will be subjected to a similar fury that was once visited upon those who denied the magic of transubstantiation.

There is a religious-style zeal to the protection of transgenderism from criticism or denial or blasphemy. The word 'transphobia' is used to demonise the belief that men cannot become women. Fighting transphobia isn't about ending discrimination against trans people — it is about silencing moral views that are now considered unacceptable; it is about turning certain beliefs into heresies. 'Transphobia' is really a new word for blasphemy. To accuse someone of 'transphobia' is to accuse them of having sinned or libelled against the new orthodoxy that says gender is fluid, some men have female brains, binaries are a myth, and so on. Make no mistake: transphobic means heretic.

Witness how feminists who question the magic of transgenderism are hounded off campuses and blacklisted by Britain's National Union of Students. These feminists are referred to by the most awful names online: bitches, cunts, whores. Or TERFs. TERF, meaning trans-exclusionary radical feminist, has become the most common insult hurled at these blasphemous women. TERFs are blacklisted by student officials. They have been physically prevented by trans activists from holding public meetings. They have been violently attacked: in 2017, trans activists assaulted a 60-year-old grandmother, or TERF, to give her the dehumanising name they gave her as they punched her in the face.

A TERF is a witch. That is really what TERF means: troublesome woman, uppity woman, defiant woman, heretic. Just as the medieval fear and fury with witches was driven by the Church's urge to root out heresy, to discover and punish unorthodox thinking, so today's blacklisting and assaulting of TERFs is driven by the new establishment's intolerance of dissent towards the new religiosity of genderfluidity. Especially among women. Religious-style wars on heresy always hate female dissenters even more than male ones. That the TERF-finders, like the witch-finders of old, hate female heretics more than male ones — more than me, for example — is testament both to the trans movement's intolerance of any view of womanhood that differs to its own elastic, eccentric view of womanhood, and also to its commonalities with earlier movements against witch-like female defiance of religious diktat.

So, recently we had the spectacle of 300 female members of the UK Labour Party resigning in protest at the party's decision to include people who were born male on all-women shortlists. And other party members, including male ones, cheered as the women left. 'Get the TERFs out', they tweeted. Cast the witches out. Expel them. Heretics not welcome. That many left-wing men laugh at these women's concerns, or approve of the censorship of their ideas, or conspire in the demonisation of them as TERFs, suggests the ideology of transgenderism has a strong streak of misogyny. Indeed, trans activism looks increasingly like misogyny in drag.

Witness, also, how criticism of the trans ideology is written off not only as wrong, but as dangerous, as morally corrupted and morally corrupting. Apparently, these people's beliefs are a kind of poison, liable to pollute souls and minds and maybe even cause young trans people to kill themselves. A certain point of view, one that says you cannot magically change sex, is imbued with awesome, devastating power, the power to kill.

This, too, is in keeping with earlier crusades against heresy. Then, as now, unorthodox thinking, whether it went against Vatican law or raised questions about Biblical scripture, was treated not only as ill informed but as ill, a sickness, and a sickness that might spread. As one historical account puts it, people and sometimes entire communities were viewed as being 'infected with heresy'. Today, that profoundly censorious idea finds expression in the war on the blasphemy of transphobia. As one headline put it recently,

'Transphobia is the mental illness, not transsexuality'. Or as a writer for the *Los Angeles Times* said, it is the critics of transgenderism who are 'truly sick'. That is, their ideas are a contagion that cause harm and sometimes death. They are infected with heresy, and they infect others with their heresy.

What we are witnessing is a classic act of demonology: the transformation of an entire group of people, trans-critical people, into demons. Through demonology, censorship and occasionally violence, the belief that you cannot magically change sex — a belief I hold to — has been turned from an acceptable point of view into a heresy you utter at your risk. I find this fast and unforgiving transformation of a moral view into a mortal sin fascinating, because it is a modern case study in the making of witches. It deserves study, this moral and physical assault on an idea, because it represents a 21st-century version of the diseasing of critical thinking that was more commonplace in darker moments in history.

As I have watched all of this unfold, I started to ask myself a question: what happens when you become a heretic? What happens when, through no fault of your own, your beliefs are deemed to be dangerous? What happens when the parameters of acceptable thinking shrink, suddenly and violently, and you find yourself outside of them, an intellectual leper? What should this newly christened heretic do?

It seems pretty clear to me that he or she has a choice. A difficult choice, but a choice nonetheless. At this point it's worth noting that heresy actually means choice. The word heresy comes from the Greek for 'choice', for 'the chosen thing'. To be a heretic is to make a choice — the wrong choice, in the view of the guardians of orthodoxy. And the choice faced by today's accidental heretics, by those who woke up one day to find that the thing they have been saying for years is now verboten, is this: you either accept your status as 'evil' and silence yourself for the supposed good of social stability; or you reject this status and continue to utter your so-called heresy because you believe, sincerely, that it is true. This is your choice, this is your heresy.

And I expect it will not surprise many of you that my advice is to do the latter: continue to speak your heresy, and damn the consequences. You should do this for two reasons. First, because it will be good for you as an individual. And secondly because it will be good for society as a whole.

Of course it isn't only trans-critical thinking that has been rebranded heresy. The industry of demonology has been working overtime of late, busy discovering new demons, busy delegitimising certain beliefs. The language of demonology is rampant in public life today. The two most common brands imposed on those judged to hold heretical beliefs are 'phobic' and 'denier'. They are fascinating terms. The first, 'phobic', speaks to the treatment of certain views as irrational fears, as forms of mental illness, essentially. And the second, denier, echoes precisely the terminology used against those who were dragged before the Inquisition. They, too, were deniers: deniers of the light of Christ.

So if you criticise trans thinking, you are transphobic. If you think gay marriage is not a good idea, and that the institution of marriage plays a specific social role best filled by heterosexual couples, you are homophobic. Criticise Islam, and you're Islamophobic. Indeed, when the Runnymede Trust first popularised the term 'Islamophobia', in the 1990s, it included in its definition any expression that treats Islam as 'inferior to Western values'. So to make a particular moral judgement, in this case that Western ideals are better than Islamic ones, is to be unstable, diseased. This is a clear example of the language of demonology being used to make a heresy out of a perfectly legitimate moral view.

Worry about mass immigration, and you're xenophobic. Oppose the EU and maybe you suffer from the mental malaise of Europhobia. One pro-EU observer says Europhobia is a species of racism that is 'alien to the postwar European culture'. And so a political perspective — opposition to the Brussels oligarchy — is refashioned as irrationalism.

Alongside the phobics are the deniers. If phobics are morally ill, deniers are straight-up sinful. The most commonly made accusation of denial is against climate-change deniers. Anyone who questions not only the science of climate change but also the political proposals put forward for dealing with environmental problems — which usually involve discouraging large-scale development — is likely to be denounced as a 'denier'. And again, their words are treated not only as wrong but as morally depraved, even as a threat to life on Earth. Their ideas are imbued with a devil-like power to corrupt and harm existence itself. So it was that one environmentalist said there should be 'international criminal tribunals' for these deniers, where they might be made to 'answer for their crimes'. That is, an Inquisition. Their words are crimes, their ideas a kind of moral pollution which might be even more dangerous than industrial pollution itself. They are heretics as surely as 'Christ deniers' were heretics.

Those who have conspired in this creation of a scientific orthodoxy that mere mortals question at their peril should reflect on the fact that science itself is heresy. Or it certainly starts as heresy. In the words of Isaac Asimov, 'Some of the greatest names in science have been... heretics. Startling scientific advances usually begin as heresies.' That science and its adherents now contribute to the policing and punishment of heresy represents an abandonment of the openness to rebuke and falsification that makes science such an important endeavour in the first place.

Phobics and deniers, everywhere. Heretics, everywhere. Sometimes their heresy is punished by law, as we have seen in Europe in recent years with the arrest and fining of those who have expressed Islamophobic thoughts or homophobic ideas. And sometimes their heresy is controlled through what John Stuart Mill called 'the tyranny of custom', where non-state social pressure is used to silence corrupted and corrupting individuals. Student officials at universities excel in the enforcement of this tyranny of custom through their drawing up of blacklists of heretical speakers, their No Platforming of trans-blasphemous women, and their promiscuous use of the brands of phobia, denier, fascist and hater to make demons of anyone who dissents from their narrow, illiberal, identitarian orthodoxy. In both cases, whether the heresies are reprimanded by law or by polite society's unforgiving demand for moral conformism, the result is the same: people feel they cannot say what they believe to be true.

But they should say it. Regardless of the consequences. First, because to censor yourself, to silence your convictions, is to conspire in the diminution of your own autonomy and even humanity. It is to confess to the sin others see in you and to punish yourself for that sin. It is to internalise the Inquisitorial mindset and save the new heresy-hunters the task of punishing you because you are willing to punish yourself. To refuse to express your deeply held belief is a terrible abdication of the moral responsibilities of the free citizen.

And the second reason you should utter your heretical beliefs is because heresy is good for society. Pretty much every liberty and comfort we enjoy is the gift of heretics. From the religious heretics who suggested the Bible should be published in English, to the scientific heretics who promoted a heliocentric view of our corner of the universe, to the political heretics who proposed that women are just as capable of political thought as men, every idea that has helped to make society a better, freer, more reasoned place started out as a form of heresy whose utterance might earn you death or expulsion from Oxford University or media ridicule.

Heresy enlivens society. It expands the parameters of acceptable thought that so many today want to shrink and control and police, and in doing so it creates the space for new and daring thinking, and for new and daring social breakthroughs. We should heed the words of Robert Ingersoll, the 19th-century American lawyer and politician and defender of free thought. He said: 'Heresy is the eternal dawn, the morning star, the glittering herald of the day. Heresy is the last and best thought. It is the perpetual New World, the unknown sea, toward which the brave all sail. It is the eternal horizon of progress. Heresy extends the hospitalities of the brain to a new thought. Heresy is a cradle; orthodoxy, a coffin.'

Heresy is a cradle. That's it. Difficult and supposedly dangerous ideas are precisely the ones you should expose yourselves to. That is the New World of thought and debate you should venture into. So stop No Platforming, stop hounding heretics off campus, stop treating ideas as diseases and disagreement as violence and dissenting speech as hate speech. Instead, say what you believe, and let others say what they believe. Express your true thoughts. Give voice even to your heretical beliefs. Here are mine: bread can never become flesh, and a man can never become a woman.

Speech at Oxford University, 8 May 2018

13

TRANS WOMEN ARE NOT WOMEN

It is the free-speech warrior's lot that he always finds himself defending tossers. Neo-fascists. Cross-burning white supremacists. Finger-wagging Islamists. Graham Linehan.

Yes, to the mugs' gallery of people that us principled believers in freedom of speech must defend, we are now obliged to add Mr Linehan: the one-time funny man and co-writer of *Father Ted* who in recent years, courtesy of the unwitting window into the soul that is Twitter, has revealed himself to be an intolerant, oafish abuser of anyone who dissents from his narrow and Brexitphobic (natch) worldview.

For Mr Linehan has now found himself on the receiving end of both police pressure and Twittermob fury simply for something he said; simply for his beliefs; simply because he dissents from the increasingly eccentric and authoritarian ideology of transgenderism.

Given that Mr Linehan himself doesn't believe in freedom of speech — consider his condemnation of Count Dankula, the Scottish meme-maker and 'shit-poster' who was outrageously arrested for filming his pet pug doing a Nazi salute — some are chuckling about the fact that he now finds himself the victim of the very PC censorship he has previously approved of.

Fine, have a laugh about that, get it out of your system. And then let's get back to defending Linehan, because even people who don't believe in freedom of speech must have their freedom of speech defended.

Linehan's speechcrime was to be trans-sceptical — or 'transphobic', to use the word preferred by trans activists and their allies, which include the police, the military, the Church, the educational establishment, the academy, and virtually every single celebrity. Such an oppressed movement!

Linehan has been getting into online spats for months with trans activists. He agrees with those feminists who argue that making it easier for men to identify as women (even referring to them as men is a transphobic hate crime, I know) is not good for women. He believes such casual, fad-like self-identification reduces womanhood to a flimsy, easily adopted thing, like a piece of clothing, and threatens to throw open previously women-only spaces — from changing rooms to all-women shortlists in party politics — to people who have penises and the XY chromosomes.

For making these points, he has been subjected to the usual bile and censure. He has been accused of hate speech. He has been branded a 'phobe' and a 'TERF' (a trans-exclusionary radical feminist), which are to 21st-century discourse what 'heretic' and 'denier' were to 15th-century discourse: means of branding people as sinners against orthodoxy, possessed of foul minds and warped souls and deserving of expulsion from the academy, politics and public life in general.

The moralistic mobbing of Linehan by the trans speech-police and its allies moved up a notch when he got into a Twitterspat with the trans activist Stephanie Hayden. He dared to refer to Stephanie as 'he' and he even 'deadnamed' her, which is when you use the name a trans person was given at birth rather than the opposite-gender name they gave themselves later in life. Using 'deadnames' is like saying 'Voldemort' in the Harry Potter universe: a serious no-no that risks conjuring up monsters (though Twitter haters and woke police officers rather than dark lords).

Extraordinarily, Linehan was given a verbal-harassment warning by the UK police for his use of male pronouns, his 'deadnaming', and his claim that Hayden is a misogynist. What's more, Hayden decided to take civil-court action against Linehan, accusing him of harassment, defamation and misuse of private information.

The intervention of actual cops into differences over transgenderism captures how intensely censorious this movement has become. Not content with having 'TERFs' harassed out of public-speaking events, or with successfully invading or closing down 15 public meetings of trans-sceptics in recent months, or with carrying out at least six incidents of violence or intimidation against feminists who oppose changes to the UK Gender Recognition Act that would make it easier for men to claim to be women, now Britain's increasingly eccentric trans activists want the police to punish 'transphobic' (read: heretical) speech.

Out of all the identitarian groups, trans activism is without question the most intolerant and the one most obsessed with linguistic policing. It wants to exercise total control over how people speak, and even think, about gender. But of course this tiny, strange movement cannot achieve this on its own. The truly worrying dynamic is the capitulation of so many cultural, political and social institutions to its Orwellian demands.

So recently, the Wellcome Collection in London, one of Britain's key health and cultural institutions, announced it was holding an event and exhibition about 'womxn'. You what? It said it used that mad, unpronounceable word in order to be more 'inclusive', in order to make it clear that all sorts of women (whisper it: even people who aren't really women) could get involved. The end result, of course, is that women are erased; the word 'women' is turned effectively into a swearword that must have an X in it so that no one sees it and feels offended. Womxn: Newspeak much?

Orwellian isn't too strong a word for what is going on. Consider the trouble Linehan and others are getting into for 'deadnaming'. If we have a situation where someone's birth name cannot be uttered, and where the police might even come after you if you do utter it, then we are conspiring in the erasure of the past itself, of historical truth, of actual, provable, documented fact.

For the fact is that trans activists were born a particular sex. And they were given a particular name. And these facts were recorded, honestly and faithfully, by public-sector workers and officials — from midwives to birth registrars — in order that society might know who its citizens are.

To erase these old names, and to allow trans-people to change their sex on their actual birth certificates, which is now happening, is to engage in an explicit act of memory-holing, as it was called in *Nineteen Eighty-Four*. It pushes down the memory hole true, recorded events. It replaces the truth — that a boy was born — with a lie: that a girl was born. It represents the complete subjugation of social norms and even historical records, truth itself, to the whims of tiny numbers of gender-confused people and the powerful institutions that bizarrely nod along to their every censorious demand.

So we have to defend Linehan. And we have to defend 'deadnaming'. For 'deadnaming' is just a Newspeak word designed to demonise the telling of historical truths. Not satisfied with seeking to control contemporary discussion and attitudes, now trans activists and their allies (all institutions, in essence) want to control the past itself. No way. The past happened, it was true, and we should not allow that to be erased and forgotten just to make some people feel better about their weird gender hang-ups.

spiked, 11 October 2018

14

THE AYATOLLAH'S VICTORY

We recently passed the 30th anniversary of the publication of Salman Rushdie's *The Satanic Verses*. It would go on to become one of the most famous novels of the 20th century thanks in large part to what happened six months following its publication: Ayatollah Khomeini issued a fatwa against Rushdie and anyone involved in publishing his work. Rushdie and his 'editors and publishers' are 'condemned to death', said Khomeini on 14 February 1989.

What is extraordinary 30 years after this allegedly blasphemous book first appeared, and close to 30 years after Khomeini issued his medieval decree, is that Khomeini has won. He is the moral victor in this despicable affair. His backward outlook carries more weight these days than the decent liberalism of secular intellectuals and literary figures like Rushdie.

No, the Ayatollah's foul call for the murder of Rushdie was not successful, and we must all remain grateful for that. But his belief that certain words and thoughts are unacceptable, unutterable, unbearable, and that anyone who holds them must be punished, is now the dominant outlook of our times. And not only in the Islamic Republic of Iran but across much of the West.

Fatwas against offensive speech are now issued daily, by the Western Twitterati as much as by Eastern religious tyrants.

Intolerance of so-called blasphemy against Islam and Muhammad is now as pronounced in trendy Western circles as it is in Islamic circles. The stunningly arrogant belief that anyone who offends one's faith or ideology or identity deserves to be severely reprimanded — the belief that motored the Ayatollah's death sentence on Rushdie — is now the central belief of virtually every new political movement in Western academic and public life.

This is the true horror of the Rushdie affair: the Rushdie side won the battle — as demonstrated in the fact that Rushdie survives and his book is still widely available — but the Khomeini side won the war. The sentiment of the fatwa defeated the principled liberalism of the fatwa's opponents. We are all Ayatollahs now.

It is striking how casually, and perhaps thoughtlessly, Western thinkers and activists now mimic Ayatollah Khomeini. He raged against Rushdie because, in his view, he had insulted 'Islam, the Prophet of Islam, and the Koran'. Now, the West's own cultural elite rages against criticism of Islam. Through the nonsense idea of Islamophobia, they demonise and even seek to destroy — in the career sense, not the life-and-death sense — anybody who insults Islam or its ideas and practices.

Witness the fury that descended upon Boris Johnson after he merely mocked Islamic dress. Or the outrage that greeted then UKIP leader Paul Nuttall's description of the slaughter at Manchester Arena in 2017 as an act of 'Islamist' violence. Or the way in which students will seek to No Platform secularists who, in their view, are too critical of Islam.

No, these people are not sentenced to death, but they are threatened with social death. To question or ridicule Islam today is to risk exclusion from the realm of acceptable thought.

Indeed, a remarkable thing happened just a few years after the Ayatollah's fatwa: Britain, the very home of Rushdie, institutionalised Ayatollah-style intolerance of criticism of Islam. In 1997, the Runnymede Trust defined 'Islamophobia' as any criticism of Islam that treats it as 'inferior to the West' or as 'unresponsive to change'. Also, if you 'reject out of hand' the 'criticisms of the West made by Islam', then you are Islamophobic.

It is important to bear in mind that this definition of Islamophobia has been embraced by the actual Metropolitan Police. The Met has a long and detailed definition of Islamophobia that includes any view of Islam as 'static', 'separate', 'other', 'irrational', 'sexist' or 'aggressive', or as a 'political ideology'. According to the police — *the police* — anyone who holds these entirely legitimate, secularist, critical views of Islam is guilty of an act of hatred, of phobia, of blasphemy, in essence.

Consider how extraordinary this is: the very police force which, for a while at least, was responsible for protecting Rushdie from the Ayatollah's murderous belief that it is unacceptable for people to insult Islam now believes it is unacceptable for people to insult Islam. The once Rushdie-protecting police force now does more to protect the extremist outlook of those who sentenced Rushdie to death — namely, the outlook that says criticism of Islam is a sin, a phobia, a sickness, a crime.

One wonders what our increasingly PC, speech-punishing police would do if the Rushdie affair happened today. Arrest rather than protect Rushdie? Charge Rushdie with a hate crime? Have a word with him about how his novel broke numerous parts of their code against Islamophobic thought and suggest he tone down these beliefs in his next work?

We live in an era of secular Ayatollahism. And it is now so entrenched that there doesn't even have to be a fatwa for someone to withdraw or destroy cultural material that might be judged to be 'Islamophobic'.

In 2008, Random House decided against publishing Sherry Jones' novel *The Jewel of Medina*, which tells the story of Muhammad's relationship with his child bride Aisha, after one academic reader said it 'might be offensive to some in the Muslim community'. Both the Barbican and Royal Court Theatre in London have in recent years self-censored plays that were critical of Islam: they effectively issued fatwas against themselves. A UK student union refused to permit the sale of *Charlie Hebdo* lest it make Muslims feel 'unsafe'.

In May 2015, mere months after the Islamist — yes, Islamist — slaughter at the offices of *Charlie Hebdo*, 242 literary figures wrote to PEN America to protest against its plan to give a courage award to the French mag. We should not be 'rewarding such expression', they said. *Charlie Hebdo*'s 'cartoons of the Prophet' only cause 'humiliation and suffering' to Muslims, they continued. This is pure Ayatollahism; it is the denunciation of a magazine for the same reason Rushdie was denounced by Khomeini — because it dared to insult Islam. Thirty years since the publication of *The Satanic Verses*, these so-called intellectuals, these supposed cultural guardians, do the Ayatollah's dirty work. They maintain his legacy. They issue the fatwas.

In a sense, we shouldn't be surprised. Even back in 1988 and 1989, Western intellectuals failed to stand shoulder-to-shoulder with Rushdie, and with freedom of expression, against the Ayatollah. No less a figure than former American President Jimmy Carter condemned Rushdie for making 'a direct insult to... millions of Muslims'. John le Carré said writers should not be free to be 'impertinent to great religions with impunity'. It is clear that the censorious PC belief that certain ways of life should never be criticised was already in the ascendant back when *The Satanic Verses* was published; now it has won out.

Ayatollahism is everywhere. Witness the rage, sometimes physical, against feminists who criticise the transgender ideology. Or the arrest of people for making offensive jokes. Or the fashion for No Platforming anyone who holds non-mainstream views. Or the branding as 'phobic' anyone who criticises mass immigration, or same-sex marriage, or, of course, Islam. No one is sentenced to death. But all of these attempts to ostracise the holders of certain views share in common with the Ayatollah's fatwa a pathetic intolerance of different thought.

Thirty years after Rushdie's novel was published, the battle isn't over. It has hardly begun. The struggle for the right of people to think what they like and say what they think, and to mock all gods, prophets, ideas and fads, remains as pressing today as it has ever been.

spiked, 1 October 2018

15

TERROR AND CENSORSHIP

Another month, another atrocity. Britain's third in three months. This time the targets were Saturday-night revellers in London Bridge and Borough. Mown down and stabbed for the crime of having fun. Killed for being free.

And almost instantly, even before we knew how many souls had perished, we saw the same craven response that follows every act of Islamist terror. 'Watch out for an Islamophobic backlash', aloof observers and leftists said.

Once again, their minds were agitated more by the thought of stupid white people saying something rude about Islam than by an act of Islamist mass murder.

Their greatest fear is always what us ill-read plebs, as they see us, will say and do after a terror attack. Even as the details of the latest outrage are unfolding on the rolling news they're taking to Twitter and the media to lecture the throng. 'Don't be mean about Islam', they snootily warn.

Not only is this a deeply patronising response that treats ordinary people as a greater threat to social stability than gangs of theocratic murderers — it's also an incredibly dangerous one.

It is becoming increasingly clear that our unwillingness to criticise Islam, to throw it open to simply the same scepticism and mockery that every other religion and ideology faces, plays into the terrorists' hands. It emboldens their belief that Islam is perfect and beyond rebuke, and that anyone who says otherwise deserves punishment.

Yes, one of the main problems we face today is not that our society is too mean about Islam, but that it flatters Islam too much.

Islam in much of the West now enjoys the same kind of moral protection from ridicule that Christianity once (wrongly) enjoyed. If you criticise the Koran or question whether women should wear the full face veil, you'll be branded 'Islamophobic' and possibly elbowed out of polite society. Student unions regularly No Platform those they judge too critical of Islam. They accuse them of 'spreading hate'. Anti-Islamophobia campaign groups like Tell MAMA trawl Twitter and the press for unkind words about Islam and log them all as evidence of a 'rising tide of hate'.

Things are so bad that our political leaders won't even use the I-word when talking about terrorism. When UKIP leader Paul Nuttall broke with this informal diktat and said 'Islamism' during a BBC General Election debate, he was rounded on by the other panellists. UK Green Party leader Caroline Lucas branded him 'completely outrageous' for suggesting recent terror attacks are 'somehow representative of Islam'. He had committed the cardinal speechcrime of our era: he said something a little bit critical of Islam.

After the Manchester Arena attack, Manchester mayor Andy Burnham said the attacker was just an 'extremist'. As legendary Mancunian Morrissey quipped: 'An extreme what? An extreme rabbit?'

Our leaders and many in the media constantly censor themselves, flat-out refusing to say anything bad about Islam. And they police the minds and words of the rest of us. This censorious privilege is not extended to any other religion. We do not avoid saying 'Catholic paedophiles' about the priests who molested children for fear of tarring all Catholics with the same brush. We happily say 'Christian fundamentalist' about people who are Christian and fundamentalist.

And yet Islam is ringfenced from tough discussion. Criticism of Islam is virtually treated as a mental illness — it's a 'phobia', and a phobia, of course, is an irrational fear. Thou Shalt Not Speak Ill Of Muhammad — the key commandment of our age.

This is incredibly dangerous. This censorious flattery of Islam is, in my view, a key contributor to the violence we have seen in recent years. Because when you constantly tell people that any mockery of their religion is tantamount to a crime, is vile and racist, you actively invite them to become intolerant. You license their intolerance. You inflame their violent contempt for anyone who questions their dogmas. You provide a moral justification for their desire to punish those who insult their religion.

From the 7/7 London bombers to the *Charlie Hebdo* murderers to Salman Abedi, who blew up the Manchester Arena, all these terrorists expressed an extreme victim mentality and openly said they were punishing us for our disrespect of Islam or our ridicule of Muhammad.

According to those who knew him, Abedi was obsessed with Islamophobia. He apparently once reported a schoolteacher over his 'Islamophobic' line of questioning about conflicts in the Middle East. When a friend of his was stabbed, Abedi was convinced it was an Islamophobic hate crime, even though there was no evidence for this. He was convinced everyone hated Islam, and that hating Islam was the worst thing in the world. Where could he have got an idea like that?

Likewise, one of the London Bridge attackers — Khuram Butt — mixed with a gang of Islamists who were incredibly sensitive and hostile to criticism of Islam. Butt appeared in the 2015 Channel 4 documentary *The Jihadists Next Door*. He and his fellow Islamist loudmouths were fans of the radical American preacher Ahmad Musa Jibril, whose finger-wagging YouTube sermons are packed with cries to 'defend Islam' against 'kuffars'.

There's a depressing, unholy marriage between the chattering class's attitude to Islam and the demands of these hotheaded radicals: both believe Islam must be defended from public questioning. Our leaders want to defend it from what they view as dim-witted tabloid-newspaper readers; Islamists want to defend it from kuffars. But the cry is the same: Islam must never be demeaned. It's wonderful. Bow down.

What really stood out in that 2015 documentary was the narcissism of the aspiring jihadists, including Butt. They publicly displayed the ISIS flag in Regent's Park. They stood on street corners telling people they would go to hell for criticising Islam (a more fiery version of being No Platformed for criticising Islam). And not many members of the public, far less officials or thinkers, confronted them and debated them. Probably for fear of being branded Islamophobic. We're not allowed to criticise Muslims, right? Forcefielding Islam from the to and fro of public debate has been a disaster. It has green-lighted Islamist intolerance.

There are no quick fixes to the terror problem, but here is a good start: we should oppose all clampdowns on offence and blasphemy and Islamophobia. All of them, whether they are legal, in the form of hate-speech laws, or informal, in the guise of Twittermobs against critics of Islam or self-censoring politicians being literally struck dumb on TV because they cannot muster up the word 'Islamist'. This will at least start the process of unravelling the Islamist victimhood narrative and its bizarre, violent, officially sanctioned sensitivity to criticism.

The response of our supposed betters to terror outrages — where they say, 'Don't blame Islam, don't criticise Islam' — is the worst response imaginable. It inflames the very religious narcissism and violent self-pity that motors many of these attacks.

Making criticism of Islam as commonplace as criticism of any other religion is the first step to robbing Islamist terrorism of its warped moral agenda. It will also send a clear message to everyone in Britain: that our society prizes freedom of speech above everything else, including your religion, your prophets, your holy book, and your feelings.

The Sun, 7 June 2017

16

WHY YOU HATE ISRAEL

Why do you hate Israel more than any other nation? Why does Israel anger you more than any other nation does? Why do Israel's military activities aggravate you and disturb your conscience and provoke you to outbursts of street protesting or Twitter-fury in a way that no other state's military activities do? These are the questions that hang darkly over today's so-called progressives. Which eat away at their self-professed moral authority, at their claims to be practitioners of fairness and equality. They are the questions to which no satisfactory answer has ever been given. So they niggle and fester, expertly avoided, or unconvincingly batted away, a black question mark over much of the modern left: why Israel?

The question has returned recently, following violent clashes on the border between the Gaza Strip and Israel. Like clockwork, with a predictability that now feels just mostly depressing, these clashes that resulted in the deaths of many protesting Palestinians magically awoke an anti-imperialist, anti-war instinct among Western observers that was notably, stubbornly, mysteriously dormant when Turkey recently laid waste to the Kurdish town of Afrin or during any of the recent Saudi barbarism visited upon the benighted people of Yemen.

A member of the IDF raises his gun and suddenly the right-minded of the West switch off Spotify, take to Twitter, engage their emotional fury, and say: 'NO.' Their political lethargy lifts, their placards are dusted down, and they remember that war and violence are bad. They even go on to the streets, as people did in London and across Europe in response to the Gaza events. This is evil, they declaim, and that question rises up again, silently, awkwardly, usually ignored: why is this evil but Turkey's sponsored slaughter of hundreds of Kurdish civilians and fighters in Afrin was not? Why Israel?

Israeli activity doesn't only elicit a response from these campaigners where Turkish or Saudi or Syrian activity does not — it elicits a visceral response. The condemnation of Israel is furious and intense, the language used about it is dark, strikingly different to the language used about any other state that engages in military activity. Israel is never just wrong or heavy-handed or a country that 'foolishly rushes to war', as protesters would say about Tony Blair and Iraq, and very occasionally about Obama and Libya, and, if they were pressed for an opinion, would probably say about the Turks and the Saudis, too. No, Israel is genocidal. It is a terrorist state, a rogue state, an apartheid state. It is mad, racist, ideological. It doesn't do simple militarism — it does 'bloodletting'; it derives some kind of pleasure from killing civilians, including children. As one observer said during the clashes at the Gaza border, Israel kills those whose only crime is to have been 'born to non-Jewish mothers'. Israel hates. This Jewish State is the worst state, the most bloodthirsty state.

Following the deaths of 18 Palestinians on the Gaza border, Glenn Greenwald denounced Israel as an 'apartheid, rogue,

terrorist state', like a man reaching for as many ways as possible to
say 'evil'. One left-wing group says Israel's behaviour at the Gaza
border confirms it is enforcing a 'slow genocide' on the Palestinians.
The 'scale of the bloodletting' is horrifying, says one radical
writer. Israel loves to draw blood. A writer for Al-Jazeera says the
clashes are a reminder that Israel has turned Gaza into 'the biggest
concentration camp on the surface of the Earth', and that question,
that unanswerable, or certainly unanswered, question, rises up once
more: why is Gaza a concentration camp but Yemen, which has
been subject to a barbaric sea, land and air blockade since 2015 that
has resulted in devastating shortages of food and medicine, causing
famine and the rampant spread of diseases like cholera, is not?

By any measurement, the blockade on Yemen is worse than any
restrictions that have been placed on Gaza. People in Gaza are not
starving to death or contracting cholera in their tens of thousands, as
Yemenis are. Yet Gaza is a concentration camp while Yemen, when
they can be bothered to comment on it at all, is a war zone. Israel is
agitated against, Saudi Arabia is not. Saudi Arabia makes war; Israel
commits 'genocide', it builds 'concentration camps', it carries out
'terrorism'. And they should know better, these Jews. That is the
subtext, always: the victims of genocide turned genocidal maniacs.

Across the mainstream media, Israeli activity is always treated
differently. The Gaza clashes were frontpage news in a way that
the worse horrors of Afrin just days and weeks earlier rarely were.
Left-leaning politicians, including leaders of the UK Labour Party,
tweet stern condemnations of Israel's shootings on the Gaza border
where they were silent, or at least more restrained, in relation to
Turkey and the Kurds. Academic and cultural institutions boycott
Israel where they do not boycott Turkey, or China, or Russia, or
America and Britain for that matter, which have done their fair share

of bad things — 'bloodletting'? — in the Middle East in recent years. That only Israel is boycotted by the self-styled guardians of the West's moral conscience, by our cultural and academic elites, constantly communicates the idea that Israel is different. It is worse. It stands above every other state in terms of wickedness and hatred and war. BDS institutionalises the idea that Israel is alien among the nations, a pock among countries, the lowest, foulest state. It is a bleak irony that BDS activists holler 'apartheid!' or 'racist!' at Israel while subjecting Israel to a kind of cultural apartheid and contributing to the ugly view of this state, this Jewish state, as the maddest state, the state most deserving of your anger and even your hatred.

There have been attempts to answer that question, that looming question of 'Why Israel?', especially following recent controversies over the expression of anti-Semitic ideas in left-wing circles, including in Jeremy Corbyn's Labour Party. But the answers have been spectacularly unconvincing. Israel deserves Western campaigners' special fury because it is backed by Western leaders, our leaders, they say. So is Turkey. And the Saudis.

Israel's repression of the Palestinians has been going on for a very long time and so it feels like a grave injustice we must address, they argue. And Turkey's war against the Kurds hasn't been going on for a long time?

Israel punishes Palestinians culturally and politically and that makes it a special case, they claim, as they throw around terms like 'apartheid' to describe life in and between Israel and the Palestinian Territories and in the process distort the reality of what happens there. But again there is Turkey, disrupting their thin, self-serving narrative. Turkey genuinely seeks to strip away the cultural heritage and language and aspiration to independence of the Kurds, and on that they say nothing, or certainly little. They don't gather outside theatres in London when Turkish actors perform there. They don't shout down Turkish violinists at the Proms. They don't demand that Turkish academics and their books be expelled from Western universities. No, only Israelis. Only them. Only those people.

There is no getting away from it: the thing that is really unique about Israel is how much they hate it. Israel stands out not because of what it does but because of how they talk about what it does: as strange, bloody, vindictive, disruptive, genocidal, this 'gang of thugs indoctrinated by an ideology that dehumanises children', as the Al-Jazeera writer described Israel this week.

Say it, why don't you. They are fascists. The victims of fascism now practice fascism. This is the sentiment behind much of the myopic focus on Israel: that the Jews now do to others what people once did to them. Even though actually they don't. Even though they do nothing that bears even the remotest resemblance to the Nazis' effort to exterminate the Jews. And yet on anti-Israel demos, placards compare Gaza to the Warsaw Ghetto, people implore the Jews to remember their own suffering, Israeli flags with swastikas on them are held up. This is not anti-imperialist, it is anti-Jewish; it is the gravest insult to say that Jews or the Jewish State are the new Nazis, and they know it is a grave insult.

The treatment of Israel as uniquely colonialist, as an exemplar of racism, as the commissioner of the kind of crimes against humanity we thought we had left in the darkest moments of the 20th century, captures what motors today's intense fury with Israel above all other nations: it has been turned into a whipping boy for the sins of Western history, a punchbag for those who feel shame or discomfort with the political and military excesses of their own nations' pasts and who now register that shame and discomfort by raging against what they view, hyperbolically, as a lingering expression of that past: Israel and its treatment of the Palestinians.

They heap every horror of the past on to Israel, hence their denunciation of it as ideological, racist, imperialistic, even genocidal — in their eyes, and courtesy of their campaigning, Israel comes to symbolise the crimes of yesteryear. So when Palestinians are killed, it is not simply a tragedy, it is not simply excessive, it is certainly not something that requires serious, nuanced discussion, including about the role of Hamas in organising such protests in order to shore up international sympathy for Palestinian victimhood. No, it is an act that reminds us of the entire history of colonialism and racial chauvinism and of concentration camps and genocide, because this is what Israel now reminds people of; they project their post-colonial guilt and scepticism about the Western project on to this tiny state in the Middle East.

The rage against Israel is actually more therapeutic than political. It is not about seriously addressing the reality of life and conflict in the Middle East, but rather is driven by the narrow needs of Western observers and activists for an entity they can fume against in order to give release to their own sense of historical and political disorientation. But the impact of this therapeutic rage, this almost primal-scream therapy against Israel, is dire. It contributes to the growing conspiratorial view that certain people, you know who they are, have a uniquely disruptive influence on international affairs, political life, and everyday safety and security.

'It isn't anti-Semitic to criticise Israel', observers say, and they are absolutely right. Every nation state must be open to criticism and protest. But if you only criticise Israel, or you criticise Israel disproportionately to every other state, and if your criticism of Israel is loaded with Holocaust imagery and talk of bloodletting, and if you boycott Israel and no other nation, and if you flatter the dark imaginings of the far right and Islamists and conspiracy theorists by fretting over a super powerful Israel Lobby, and if the sight of an Israeli violinist is too much for you to stomach, then, I'm sorry, that has all the hallmarks of anti-Semitism.

spiked, 11 April 2018

17

GAY CAPITALISM

You couldn't have asked for a better, more hi-res snapshot of the state of supposedly radical politics.

It was a Saturday, the sun was out, and two very different political gatherings were taking place. In the North of England, there was the annual Durham Miners' Gala, which has been going since 1871. Former miners, brass bands, trade unionists and working-class families gathered to celebrate — or more accurately, commemorate — the labour movement and its many achievements. In London, at the same time, Pride was sprawling through the streets. Gay-rights activists and their 'allies' gathered to celebrate themselves. In an orgy of colour and noise, they advertised not so much their achievements as their characteristics; not their work, but their play; not what they do — which won't be digging for coal — but who they are. The difference between Durham and Pride tells us an incredibly important story about the fall of radical politics.

Pride is an increasingly bizarre spectacle of self-regard. It started life, in 1972, as a positive cry for gay liberation. It was a gathering of gay men and lesbians demanding greater autonomy and the dismantling of laws that still punished certain forms of gay sex even following the partial decriminalisation of homosexuality in Britain in 1967.

But in recent years it has become more about identity than autonomy; more a therapeutic demand for validation than a political cry for liberation; more an exercise in collective narcissism than collective agitation. And it's one the bourgeoisie has completely fallen in love with. Pride is now awash with capitalist cash. Recent sponsors have included Barclays, Starbucks, Tesco, Virgin, Vodafone and NBC Universal. Corporations fall over each other to pump the money they make on the backs of the working classes into this gathering of middle-class identitarians. The same capitalist class that contributed to the crushing of the mining industry in places like Durham now throws its filthy lucre at Pride in London.

Some older gay-rights activists, including Peter Tatchell, have criticised the corporatisation of Pride. Tatchell complains that 'the ideals of LGBT equality are barely visible' anymore, and instead we have a party-like event that 'big corporations see as a PR opportunity to fete LGBT consumers'. But these criticisms miss the mark somewhat. It's not that Pride has been hijacked by big business keen to tap into the Pink Pound. It's that in playing a key role in institutionalising the politics of self-regard, in assisting with the shifting of the radical political focus from the economy to identity, from questions of power to issues of esteem, Pride lends itself beautifully to the reorganisation of 21st-century capitalist society in a way that benefits those in power.

Pride and its participants haven't simply become the targets of capitalism; Pride *is* capitalism. Pride is the new face of capitalism, a glossy, pink manifestation of a new bourgeois ideology that seeks to pacify the populace through depoliticising the economy and politicising lifestyle and culture instead.

The differences between something like the Durham Miners' Gala and Pride are instructive here. Sadly, the annual Durham event looks increasingly like a museum piece, almost an historical re-enactment of struggles that simply do not take place today. There are no coalminers in Durham any more. There are no deep coal mines left in Britain, in fact. The last one, in Kellingley in North Yorkshire, closed in 2015.

As to the trade unionism the Durham gathering celebrates, that, too, is on its way out. Recent figures showed that trade-union membership has fallen to an 'all-time low' in Britain. In 2015 alone, unions shed 275,000 members. In 2016, just 81,000 workers took strike action, the lowest number since records began in 1893. However, what the Durham gala marks, what it looks back on, is important: that old demand by working people for greater power over their lives, for changes to the political and economic system for the benefit of those who labour for a living. Their call was for control and change. And their activism from the 1870s onwards helped to make life in Britain better than it otherwise would have been.

Contrast this with Pride — or with any of the other identity-based movements, or pseudo-movements, of the 21st-century, whether it's trans activism, 'SJWs' on campus, the new media feminism, or the rise of a victim-orientated politics of black identity. These new groups do not seek power, but pity. They do not challenge officialdom so much as demand its recognition, insist that it validate their minority status and acknowledge their allegedly fragile existential state. Rather than seeking autonomy from the state or the free market, they agitate for the approval of these institutions.

So new media feminists get incredibly excited over corporate advertising campaigns that recognise the importance of giving girls a leg-up, and trans activists continually demand that the state more closely monitor and punish expressions of 'transphobia' (which are often just criticisms of the politics of transgenderism). These are movements for dependence — on state validation, on free-market flattery, on the protections offered by censorship — not independence.

Indeed, the politics of identity doesn't challenge oppression but rather commodifies it. It makes it into a must-have. Oppression is no longer a state of being that must be overthrown but a condition people envy and desire. As the American political theorist Wendy Brown says, the victim sensibility is now a highly prized asset, or commodity, in late capitalist society. To such an extent that this new victim-oriented identity politics doesn't seek to overcome 'pain' but rather welcomes it (or invents it). 'Politicised identity... makes claims for itself only by entrenching, restating, dramatising and inscribing its pain in politics; it can hold out no future — for itself or others — that triumphs over this pain', writes Brown.

A perverse consequence of this pain-maintaining identity politics is that it 'naturalises capitalism', says Brown, and in fact becomes reliant on what she refers to as capitalism's 'wounded attachments'. So identity politics is explicitly anti-change, even anti-progress, because to overhaul those aspects of capitalist society that put pressure on certain groups would mean robbing those groups of the pain that they continually restate and dramatise, and through which they garner moral authority and state support in this therapeutic era. Bizarrely, oppression must now be preserved — or sought out, even where it does not exist — rather than defeated.

This is why the capitalist class loves the politics of identity. This is why it loves Pride. Because not only do these things pose no challenge whatsoever to the economic or political status quo — they are actually deeply devoted to the maintenance of the status quo. The capitalist elite is more than happy to support the annual demonstration of self-regard and dramatised oppression that is Pride because flattering this new, pseudo-leftish politics of victimhood is a small price to pay for the new order in which questions of class, wealth and power have been utterly demoted by politicised identity.

And so we reach the perverse situation where the identity politics of middle-class progressives is funded by capitalists who continue to exploit the working class. They recognise that the key dynamic of the politics of identity is its decommissioning — or rather its superseding — of a politics that they found genuinely disturbing and dangerous: class politics. That old politics which the Durham gala remembers.

This is the key difference between the old and new radical politics: the question of transcendence. In the past, the more radical left, at least, was concerned not with celebrating or even maintaining the working-class identity but rather with ending it. This was a way of life that could be overcome through the radical transformation of society. The new identitarian left has no such vision of transcendence and instead devotes itself to managing relations and speech between individuals and groups so that no one's wounds are ever made worse than they need to be. Far from Corbynism representing a challenge to this politics of identity, and a resuscitation of the old labourist outlook, we may soon find that it will in fact add the final touch to the historic decommissioning of class through its treatment of the working class itself as just another identity group whose wounds must be tended to — by the welfare state, by therapeutic intervention, by institutionalised recognition of their 'vulnerablity'. And this will be a final victory for a capitalist class delighted that questions of power have been replaced by a new elitist imperative of managing people's self-esteem.

spiked, 12 July 2017

18

YOU ARE NOT MENTALLY ILL

One of the great media myths of the 21st century is that there's a taboo against talking about mental illness. Please. Then how come I can't open a newspaper or flick through my TV channels or browse social media without seeing someone go into grisly depth, often replete with sad selfies, about his latest bout of mental darkness?

Far from taboo, having a mental illness, and talking about your mental illness, is all the rage. It's the latest must-have. You're no one unless you've had a mental episode. And I find this transformation of mental illness into a fashion accessory far worse than the old treatment of it as a taboo (which was very bad).

The latest people who have set out to 'break the taboo' on talking about mental illness – the worst enforced taboo in history! – are Princes William and Harry. As part of their Heads Together campaign they want to shatter the stigma around mental health (lads, there's no stigma) by getting people, especially younger people, to open up about their mental travails.

Prince William even did a FaceTime chat with Lady Gaga to raise awareness about mental ill-health. Under the hashtag #OKtoSay, tweeters are being encouraged to gab about their ups and downs. It's time to trade the 'stiff upper lip' for a wobbly lip, stoicism for confessed vulnerability, said William.

Now, anyone who raises so much as a peep of criticism of campaigns like this runs the risk of being branded a heartless bastard. So let me make it clear that I appreciate that William and Harry had a horrendous experience early in life, with the death of their mother, and it undoubtedly shaped them enormously. I respect them for coming through it in good moral shape. But I'm not buying the idea that their mental-health campaign is brave or necessary. I think it's dangerous.

It's dangerous firstly because it springs from and reinforces the weird 21st-century trend for actively inviting people to define themselves as mentally ill. Everything from exam stress to general anxiety to feeling up one day and down the next – which used to be called 'moods' but is now called 'bipolar disorder' – is being recategorised as a mental illness or disorder.

Everyday emotions and experiences have been co-opted into the field of mental health. You think you're shy? Nope, you have social anxiety disorder. Do you have an awkward friend? Maybe he has Asperger's. Finding it hard to cope with your workload? Check out the Workplace Stress and Anxiety Disorder Survey — this is a real thing — to find out if really you are mentally ill.

Virtually all of life's struggles and people's personality quirks are being medicalised. And in some cases treated: Britain is said to be in the grip of a 'psychiatric drug epidemic', as the number of prescriptions for mental-health drugs rose by an astonishing 500% between 1992 and 2014. It's like something out of Huxley's *Brave New World,* in which people are given a mind drug that suppresses their 'malice and bad tempers'.

And people actively seek a diagnosis. A few years ago, a psychiatrist told the BBC that patients come to her saying, 'I want to be bipolar'. She said the desire for a mental-illness diagnosis often reflects 'a person's aspiration for higher social status'. Yes, you can now boost your standing in respectable society by having a mental illness. This is how cool it has become to be mentally ill.

The dire impact of the must-have mental illness is most clear among the young. I can't remember the last time I met a student who didn't claim to have a mental illness of some kind. A few weeks of stress over their exams and they think they're Jack Nicholson in *One Flew Over the Cuckoo's Nest*. They post long social-media confessions of mental ill-health and everyone says 'How brave', overlooking that it's really not brave to do something everyone else is doing; to say 'I am mentally ill' in a world in which you can't swing a tote bag in Waterstone's without hitting 20 books about being mentally ill. Everyone's mentally ill; you aren't special – you're boring.

The problem here is that people are being told it's cool not to be able to cope, to embrace the identity of fragility. They are invited to think of themselves as incapable, to build their personality around being pathetic. That's terrible. This ultimately expresses society's inability to provide people with a sense of purpose in their lives, with a moral framework for making sense of the world and our place within it, and this gives rise to a situation where people come to understand the problems they face not as social, political or economic, but as psychic.

The other really bad thing about the mental-illness fashion is what it does to mental-health services: it clogs them up. It distracts the attention of doctors away from those who are genuinely in need: the clinically depressed, the schizophrenic, the suicidal. I'm sorry, but I think it is awful that we live in such self-obsessed, entitled times that people stressed about work or in a very bad temper are jumping the queue over people in true despair. Get out of the waiting room, for heaven's sake.

We shouldn't ditch the stiff upper lip; we should rehabilitate it, and encourage the young in particular to exercise it. Having a stiff upper lip doesn't mean being an arrogant twit who thinks nothing in life ever touches him – it simply means believing that you have the moral and mental wherewithal to cope with things, even when they get difficult. It means being an adult, being autonomous, and emphasising your strengths, not your weaknesses. The real taboo today is against saying, 'I can cope with life, with the help of my friends, and I refuse to define myself as weak or ill'. Let's break that taboo. Now that would be brave.

spiked, 20 April 2017

19

WOKE MONARCHY

Congratulations, Harry and Meghan. I hope you have a long marriage. What I hope doesn't last quite as long is this Woke Monarchy your nuptials apparently herald.

Everyone's raving about how the monarchy has finally landed in the 21st century, shaking off its old, oh-so-white ways to become a modern, multicultural outfit that signals to all Brits, whatever their hue, that they are much-loved. It's such a patronising mission, as patrician as any earlier big royal event that was likewise justified as a means of making the plebs feel fleetingly good about their lives.

It was a fascinating wedding. And a nice one, sure. The chamber music was lovely. As was the Kingdom Choir's rendition of *Stand By Me*. The sight of David Beckham making smalltalk with Sir Nicholas Soames was hilarious. But the whole thing was just so knowing and strained. It was a carefully orchestrated stab at projecting a new image of monarchy that ended up as a confused pageant that was neither one thing nor the other.

The new aristocrats — slebs like Clooney, Oprah and Elton — awkwardly rubbed shoulders with old aristocrats most of us would struggle to name. The black American episcopalian preacher was a hit with the crowds but left the Queen and Princess Anne visibly perplexed. The presence of the black choir was celebrated as a herald of the New Britain and yet everyone ended up singing 'God Save the Queen', as they always must, because the Queen, for all this institution's much trumpeted modernisation, is still an instrument of God to lead the British people and various other Commonwealth peoples.

The wedding captured but of course did zilch to resolve a simmering tension in the upper echelons of British society. It brought together modern-day 'kweens' (Serena, Amal, Posh Spice) with the actual Queen, leaving us unsure who we're meant to bow to these days. The media talking point — and clearly the guiding principle of Prince Harry's team — was 'inclusivity', yet the monarchy remains the least inclusive organisation in the land. You literally have to have been created by a particular person's sperm to have a place in it. The rest of us have more chance of being included in a mission to Mars than we do of becoming members of the 'inclusive' House of Windsor.

It all spoke to a monarchy at sea, and to a political class — they always have their fingers in events like these — uncomfortable with Britain's old traditions but unable to give meaning to its new ones. The most bizarre idea is that Meghan's arrival will make the monarchy more representative. The monarchy isn't meant to be representative. It's meant to be the opposite of representative. It is supposed to stand above both grubby politics and us mere mortals to embody a superhuman moral aura that might steer the nation. This inherently anti-representative, aloof nature of monarchism is precisely why some of us would prefer to live in a Republic of Britain. Making the monarchy inclusive is political surrealism.

What people mean when they talk about a new 'representative' monarchy is that it will make ordinary people, Her Majesty's apparently confused subjects, feel good about themselves. The fact that the royal family's latest addition is mixed-race will apparently open the eyes of the throng to the importance of multiculturalism. Meghan could 'change Britain's attitude to race', says one headline. 'A new era dawns', says the *New York Times*, telling us that 'after generations of aristocratic matches, [this union] more closely reflects modern Britain'. (It forgets that middle-class Kate Middleton also wasn't an aristocratic match.) Commentators tell us black Brits will now feel like worthy citizens, and white Brits will get a lesson in inclusivity. 'From now on, it will be impossible to argue that being black is somehow incompatible with being British', says one columnist.

The paternalistic presumptions are astonishing. They really believe black Brits have been waiting for royal approval before feeling part of the British nation? And white Brits need to see a black woman standing next to Prince Harry in order to realise black people are acceptable? Black communities are seen as child-like victims in need of a dark-skinned duchess to make them feel better, and white people as latent racists whose ugly passions must be kept in check with regular photos of our monarchical betters being nice to a mixed-race woman. The post-traditionalist elites have a pretty traditional contempt for the plebs.

We're back to the idea of the 'magic' of monarchy. The key aspect of monarchy is its 'theatrical elements', said Bagehot in *The English Constitution*; theatre that might 'appeal to the senses'. Same now, it seems, though today the theatre is one of 'inclusivity' justified as a means of repressing people's bad, racist senses and teasing out our good, multiculturalist ones. It is striking how much the PC worldview echoes the aristocratic one. Both see representation in hereditary rather than democratic terms: Meghan is celebrated for

the accident of her birth to mixed-race parents just as the Queen is
the Queen because of the accident of her siring by George VI. Both
marshal 'theatre' to massage the plebs' 'senses', from the stiff theatre
of the Queen's coronation that was designed to pluck up postwar
Blighty to the virtue-signalling of the Harry and Meghan pageant.
And both bristle at real representation: democratic representation.
Instead, the old aristocracy prefers the rule of the high-born while
the new aristocracy prefers the influence of celebrity, expertise and
technocracy over government by the pesky, Brexity people.

So spare us this Woke Monarchy, and this 'New Britain' in which
theatre is still deployed to educate the throng and where we're all
expected to respond positively to identitarian gestures. Because it
strikes some of us that these woke elites might be as patronising as
the old elites, and possibly more so.

spiked, 20 May 2018

20

THE FURY OF THE ELITES

Hell hath no fury like an establishment spurned. If you didn't know this already, you certainly know it now, following the British people's vote for Brexit. A whopping 17.4million of us voted to cut our nation's ties with the European Union, against 16.1million who voted to stay. And we did so against the advice of most of the political class, media experts, the Brussels bureaucracy, the International Monetary Fund, President Barack Obama, and virtually every other Western leader. Most shockingly of all, against the advice of celebs: not even Benedict Cumberbatch's earnest, crumpled face could make us want to stay. We defied them all. We rejected every EU-loving overture from the great and good and well-educated. And boy, are they mad.

Ever since this modern-day peasants' revolt took place — Britain's poor and working classes voted for Brexit in far large numbers than the well-to-do and well-connected — the political and media elites have rained damnation upon the little people. Their language has crossed the line from irritated to full-on misanthropic. They're calling into question the ability of ordinary people to rationally weigh up hefty political matters, and are even suggesting the referendum result be overturned in the name of the 'national interest'.

David Lammy, a Member of Parliament representing the Labour Party, has been most explicit. He says we must 'stop this madness' and 'bring this nightmare to an end'. The nightmare he's talking about is people voting for things he doesn't agree with. He says the people's will must now be overridden by a 'vote in Parliament'. It's terrifying that an elected MP doesn't seem to know how democracy works.

Peter Sutherland, a United Nations Special Representative, likewise thinks the Brexit vote 'must be overturned', because voters were led astray by a 'distortion of facts'. UN officials normally slam the thwarting of a people's will; now they promote it.

And Tony Blair's former spindoctor says he has 'lawyers on the case' to see if a legal challenge can be mounted against the masses and their dumb decision. Lawyers v the People: bring it on.

Nicola Sturgeon, leader of the Scottish National Party and First Minister of Scotland, has threatened to veto Brexit as it works its way through Parliament. This is a woman whose party received 1.5million votes in the General Election last year, now saying she will usurp the will of 17.4million Brits who said screw-you to the E.U.

Media commentary, meanwhile, has become positively unhinged and Victorian in its attitude to the throng. *Guardian* columnist Polly Toynbee, finding that she didn't like some of the pro-Brexit arguments, said Brexiteers have 'lifted several stones' and let out a 'rude, crude… extremism'. We all know what lives under stones. An *Observer* columnist, perusing the Brexit chatter, said 'it is as if the sewers have burst'. Over at the *New Statesman,* house magazine of the British left, a columnist claims it was 'the frightened, parochial lizard-brain of Britain [that] voted out, out, out'.

Reptiles, insects, shit flowing from the busted sewer of bad ideas

— this is how the media elite views the minds and actions of Brexit people.

A recurring theme in the elitist rage with the pro-Brexit crowd has been the idea that ordinary people aren't sufficiently clued-up to make big political decisions. We have witnessed a 'populist paean to ignorance', says one observer. Apparently populist demagogues — like Nigel Farage, leader of the UK Independence Party, and Boris Johnson, everyone's favourite bumbling, toffish politician — preyed on the anxieties of the little people and made them vote for something bad and stupid. For these little people, 'fear counts above reason; anger above evidence', opined a writer for the *Financial Times*. A writer for the *Guardian* suggested that for anti-EU types, emotions 'play a larger part than rationality'.

This idea that the less well-educated sections of society are ripe for exploitation by emotion-stoking demagogues is not new. It's the prejudice that has motored most elite campaigns against the expansion of democracy. The Chartists, Britain's brilliant 19th-century warriors for universal male suffrage, encountered this nasty prejudice all the time. Their critics insisted that 'the lower orders of the people' do not have a 'ripened wisdom', and therefore they are 'more exposed than any other class in the community to be tainted by corruption, and converted to the vicious ends of faction'. Others said that 'spouters at the meetings of the working classes' could easily exploit the 'astonishing ignorance and credulity on the part of the hearers'.

The Chartists raged against such nasty elitism. How horrified they would be to know that, 150 years later, it is back with a vengeance, in the idea that the scared British people are allegedly ripe for canny right-wing operators to manipulate.

Indeed, much of the elitist rage with the masses who voted for Brexit echoes a longstanding suspicion of democracy. Among the upper echelons of society there has never been a willing acceptance of the idea that ordinary people should have an equal say in political life. As John Carey notes in his classic 1992 book *The Intellectuals and the Masses,* late 19th- and early 20th-century thinkers and writers feared nothing more than mass democracy. Carey describes how numerous European writers and artists warmed to Nietzsche's view of democracy as a 'tyranny of the least and the dumbest'.

Sure, in these politically correct times, few would use such ugly language to describe ordinary people. But the angry petition calling for a second referendum on the EU, the various middle-class marches on Parliament to demand that MPs reject Brexit, and the suggestion that young people in particular have had their futures destroyed by 'some of the oldest and whitest people on Earth [voting] against the monsters in their heads' — as one columnist put it — all speak to an elitist disgust with the 'tyranny of the least and the dumbest', and to a desire to prevent their democratically stated views from becoming reality.

This is as ugly an anti-masses sentiment as I can remember. And the consequences of it are likely to be dire. Ordinary people are effectively being told they're too dumb for politics. And democracy is being treated as a negotiable commodity that can be cast aside if the stupid public makes the wrong decision. This is a species of tyranny. The mask has slipped. Our normally polite elite, feeling bruised and aloof after Britain's referendum, has dispensed with its usual platitudes about 'respecting all views', and shown that beneath the veneer there lurks an ancient fury with the least and the dumbest; with the masses; with the people.

Reason, 27 June 2016

21

AVENGING BILL LEAK

We have mourned Bill Leak. Now we must avenge him. The time for tears has passed. It's anger we need now.

Anger at his persecution by that unholiest of alliances: violent-minded Islamists and joyless, cartoon-burning leftists. The former having forced Bill out of his home with menaces and threats after he dared to draw Muhammad, the latter having raged and spluttered against him for daring to defy their lazy, illiberal consensus on everything from environmentalism to gay marriage to PC.

Anger that the very wing of the Australian state that claims to act in the name of human rights — the bloated, ridiculous Human Rights Commission — did not defend Bill's human right to say and draw whatever he damn well pleased, but instead hounded him for being 'offensive'. Did not utter a word in defence of his freedom but instead sided with those throwbacks to the Dark Ages who thirsted for the curbing of his freedom. A pincer movement of bureaucrats and barbarians, of the officious and the vicious, with Bill their quarry.

Anger that a nation descended from larrikinism, marvelled over by that self-styled gruff man of letters DH Lawrence as a country in which 'nobody is supposed to rule, and nobody does rule', did not celebrate Bill but instead wrung its hands over him. Worried he was going too far; worried he was too outspoken; worried he was a tad too Australian.

Avenge is a strong word, I know. It conjures up images of gangs of swordsmen visiting retribution upon their persecutors. That's not what I mean. Avenge comes from *vindicare* — to vindicate. That's what I mean. Bill must be vindicated, and the freedoms he both defended in speeches and lived every day — the freedom to doubt, to speak, to offend — fought for. Dry your tears; we have work to do.

My first response when I received an email from Nick Cater telling me Bill had died was great sadness. Just 24 hours earlier I had emailed him to congratulate him on the launch of his book *Trigger Warning: Deplorable Cartoons* and to remind him he's my hero. With typical humility he fired back: 'And you're mine!'

Bill was one of the nicest people I've met. Whether he was talking me through Aussie history at the Art Gallery of New South Wales or regaling me over drinks (him: water, me: beer) with tales of his decades of encounters with Oz's most colourful political and cultural characters, his conversation buzzed with comedy and humanism and intellect. You came away cleverer and cheerier.

He once dropped me off at the Surry Hills apartment I was staying in and we were sat outside in his car for two hours, gabbing. 'I've gotta go', he kept saying, but didn't. He told me that when Tanya Plibersek was the nannying Health Minister he designed some warning labels for alcohol that he was on the cusp of emailing to her but then thought better of it. One said: 'DRINKING CAN MAKE YOU SHIT YOURSELF.' I thought it was about the funniest pricking of the arrogance of the paternalists I'd ever heard. I wish he'd sent them.

The truth of Bill runs so counter to the intolerant left's depiction of him as to be surreal. They viewed him as cruel simply because he had the audacity to rip the mick out of their eco-pieties and virtue orgies and allergy to liberty. I can think of few people less cruel than Bill, or more big-hearted. His motive was humanism, his instinct was scepticism, his belief was that ordinary people would probably make a better fist of running their lives than any ponce or Plibersek ever could. He trusted people.

But slowly, my sorrow at his death has given way to ire over how he was treated in his final years; over the Leakphobia of the chattering classes; over their defaming and shaming and hounding of Bill simply because he refused to be constrained by the ever-tightening parameters of their Acceptable Thinking.

Bill dealt with his harassers with good humour and ridicule. But they got to him. I've been rereading his emails from the past couple of years and it's a bloody painful experience. 'They're actually trying to hunt me down and kill me', he said of the Islamists who in 2015 persecuted him for drawing Muhammad. When the HRC took the depraved decision to investigate his cartoon of an Aborigine dad, he wrote to me about 'these smiley face fascists trying to ruin my life'. Of the leftists cheering on the HRC, he said 'they're going at me with all guns blazing'.

In December he sent me his submission to the Inquiry into Freedom of Speech — a searing, brilliant argument that freedom of speech is 'the hallmark of a robust liberal democracy' — with this note: 'I'm knackered. The past few months have been really draining.' It's hard to read that now, knowing that three months later he would be dead.

Let's make no bones of this: Bill was subjected to an Inquisitorial persecution. No, there were no pointy-hatted Bible-bashers or stakes being lit. But through the menaces of Islamists and the Stalinist cries for *The Australian* to dump him and the HRC's vile hauling of him to account for himself, a man was afflicted for his thoughts, hectored for his ideas, made 'knackered' and 'drained' for daring to express what he believed to be true. Censorship is cruel. Witch-hunts are implicitly violent. They take a toll on their victims. And they took a toll on Bill.

This makes me angry. It should make you angry too. Those who knew Bill will remember him fondly, but we should avenge him furiously. The oppressions he was subjected to by religious hotheads and nasty bureaucrats speak to the low esteem in which freedom is held today. Bill dared to live and speak freely, even as the consequences for doing so grew more severe. Let's now vindicate him by demanding the repeal of Section 18C and the abolition of the foul oligarchy of the HRC, and by challenging every religious, political and cultural figure that uses menaces or law to try to chip away at freedom of speech. Let's ensure Australia once again becomes a country where 'nobody rules' on what you can say, and where larrikinism — better still, Leakism — flourishes.

The Spectator, 18 March 2017

A Duty to Offend:
Selected Essays by Brendan O'Neill

ISBN: 9781925138764, Paperback, 130 pages, $19.95 (AUD)
Published in 2015

Described by the *Daily Mail* as 'one of Britain's leading left-wing thinkers' and by the *Guardian* as an 'obnoxious intellectual wind-up merchant', essayist and bruiser Brendan O'Neill is no stranger to controversy. In this selection of recent essays, he explores everything from free speech to feminism, porn to Thomas Paine, coal (good) to Chomsky (bad). Fuelled by humanism, the essays put the case for a new enlightenment, and for rediscovering our faith in 'the dignity and excellence of man'.

www.connorcourtpublishing.com.au

Lightning Source UK Ltd.
Milton Keynes UK
UKHW010624160720
366640UK00001B/272